Before Bemberg

Before Bemberg

Women Filmmakers in Argentina

MATT LOSADA

Rutgers University Press
New Brunswick, Camden, and Newark, New Jersey, and London

Library of Congress Cataloging-in-Publication Data

Names: Losada, Matt, author.
Title: Before Bemberg : women filmmakers in Argentina / Matt Losada.
Description: New Brunswick : Rutgers University Press, [2020] |
 Includes bibliographical references, filmography, and index.
Identifiers: LCCN 2019048886 | ISBN 9781978814554 (hardback) |
 ISBN 9781978814547 (paperback) | ISBN 9781978814561 (epub) |
 ISBN 9781978814578 (mobi) | ISBN 9781978814585 (pdf)
Subjects: LCSH: Women in the motion picture industry. | Women motion
picture producers and directors—Argentina—Biography. | Motion pictures—
 Argentina—History—20th century. | Motion picture
 industry—Argentina—History—20th century.
Classification: LCC PN1995.9.W6 L68 2020 | DDC 791.4302/30820982—dc23
LC record available at https://lccn.loc.gov/2019048886

A British Cataloging-in-Publication record for this book
is available from the British Library.

Copyright © 2020 by Matt Losada
All rights reserved
No part of this book may be reproduced or utilized in any form or by any means,
electronic or mechanical, or by any information storage and retrieval system, without
written permission from the publisher. Please contact Rutgers University Press,
106 Somerset Street, New Brunswick, NJ 08901. The only exception to this
prohibition is "fair use" as defined by U.S. copyright law.

♾ The paper used in this publication meets the requirements of the
American National Standard for Information Sciences—Permanence of Paper
for Printed Library Materials, ANSI Z39.48-1992.

www.rutgersuniversitypress.org

Manufactured in the United States of America

L'homme qui a le plus de sympathie pour la femme ne connaît jamais bien sa situation concrète.
—Simone de Beauvoir

Contents

	Introduction	1
1.	A History of the Gendered Division of Labor in Argentine Cinema	9
2.	Eva Landeck	50
3.	Beauvoir before Bemberg	79
	Acknowledgments	143
	Filmography	145
	Notes	147
	Works Cited	163
	Index	179

Before Bemberg

Introduction

In the twenty-first century, women in Argentina have enjoyed greater access to creative participation in filmmaking than ever before, but if we look toward the past and ask about the precursors of today's filmmakers, into view comes a long-standing gendered division of labor that, though attenuated, persists in the present. Prior to the emergence of María Luisa Bemberg, who in a brief, busy career directed six feature films after 1980 that were resoundingly successful both in Argentina and internationally, very few women directed. Because those few who did direct remain little known, this book sets out to look beyond Bemberg, to trace the untold stories of these women, and, more important for their full valorization, to closely consider the films they made, in order to account for what could today be called the prehistory of the creative participation of women in Argentine cinema.

The book opens with an overview of the historical presence of women in the so-called creative roles in filmmaking. It begins with the 1910s, when several women produced and directed, then progresses through the classical cinema of the studios (roughly 1933–1956), when women were excluded from participation in the creative roles of scriptwriting and direction, and on to the 1960s, when many women took advantage of the opportunities presented by a boom in short filmmaking. Then the book closely examines the few features made by women during the 1960s and 1970s, which, without exception, continue to suffer critical neglect.

The directors of these films, Vlasta Lah, María Herminia Avellaneda, María Elena Walsh, and Eva Landeck, found the celluloid ceiling resistant, and none made more than two films in Argentina.[1] Most worked independently of studios, a positioning that granted them a great degree of creative freedom from the usual commercial concerns of producers. Their films are extraordinary in many ways, from formally inventive explorations of the perspectives of female characters, to daring denunciations of authoritarianism and censorship, to radical critiques of the cofunctioning of modern consumer capitalism and traditional gender order. My approach to these filmmakers will be to examine each as an auteur with marginal status with respect to established commercial filmmaking. I do not use the term "auteur" to refer necessarily to how a filmmaker's identity is manifested in her work—autobiographical elements, real presence on film, or even narrative focalization on female characters—but instead to the fact that her films are generated by an individual or a small team, rather than a studio.[2] Such an approach underlines the unique contribution of each in terms of production models that allow them to address singular formal and thematic concerns.

Although it is of course problematic to argue for generalizations about an essential relationship between the gender of directors and the films they make, an examination of the few films made by women reveals that they frequently, but not necessarily, explored areas of human experience usually left untouched by films that did not include women in creative roles. Given the masculine predominance in such roles in Argentine cinema, it is not surprising that the representation of women was less often as subject—of vision, of psychology, of desire—than as object. Especially during the classical studio period of 1933 to 1956, the representation of women tended toward homogeneity, and they were looked at, contemplated, and desired, but less often looked, contemplated, or desired. These representations tended to conform to traditional models that emphasized women's role in the home and the family, with maternity as destiny, whether fulfilled or not (Conde 2005, 9).[3] The reasons for such representations were similar to those of Hollywood:

an industrial logic of production that required mass consumption, feared alienating certain sectors of the viewership or pressure groups, and was thus hesitant to stray from the known, safe set of conventional representations.[4] These commercial demands resulted in an avoidance of provocative ideas around gender in classical film that was compounded by the historic predominance, even near monopoly, of men in the roles of producers, writers, directors, critics, and censors. As Mariana Inés Conde writes, "The dearth of women involved in [classical cinema] production did not allow it to capture another tone or, perhaps, other problematics or the simple multiplication of points of view, which always produces discomfort and questioning" (2005, 9). By contrast, an examination of the very few films directed by women between 1960 and 1980 finds several instances of a "multiplication of points of view" that might have brought discomfort not only to the spectator but also to critics, censors, and producers.

These films also articulate unique perspectives on the world; thus, in my examination of them I focus on ways in which they break with the established representational conventions of Argentine cinema. The most obvious is the use of female characters as narrative focalizers and, by extension, the representation of their subjectivity. In the classical cinema, as well as in the commercial cinema made since the demise of the studios, women seldom focalize narration, and with even less frequency is the viewer prompted to identify with them.[5] So one focus of this book is the representation of female subjectivity in films made by women directors, which leads inevitably to the representation of female desire. Sexual desire on the part of female characters was generally portrayed as antisocial in the classical cinemas the world over, with desiring women conventionally punished by suffering or death by the end of a film, while a less immediately painful destiny usually awaited the more chaste female characters. The most well-known rupture with these conventions is seen in the work of Bemberg in the 1980s, in which the tribulations of independent-minded and sexually desiring women are caused expressly by an oppressive patriarchy, but it would be difficult to argue that it is mere coincidence that the first film directed by a woman in four decades, Vlasta Lah's *Las furias* (1960), also explored the theme of female sexual desire.

So rather than simply cataloging women's participation in film production, this book asks about the creative impact of women and what it brings to the films themselves, as well as to their reception. The work of most of these filmmakers, as well as the fact of their female authorship, has had little impact on the Argentine cinema field more generally. This can be attributed to several interrelated factors. First, since only one of these women directed for an established commercial producer, their films did not enjoy the ready distribution that studio product had. The few films made by women were, then, already marginalized and little known on their original release; as a result, they have more readily fallen outside of recently opened digital channels of distribution, remaining difficult to find and ignored by critics and scholars. Today, even in scholarship eager to call attention to women filmmakers, they remain in the shadows, usually limited to anecdotal mentions. This lack of historical importance is another of my motivations for studying these films. Ideally this book will contribute to their reintegration into film history at a doubly significant moment, one in which the dedication of archivists, preservationists, and exhibitors has made it possible to focus new light on the hidden corners of the cinematic archive at the same time that movements to eliminate gender-based injustices and violence are surging in Argentina and elsewhere. Such a recuperation would allow today's cinephiles and scholars to access a more complete history and acknowledge the past difficulties and possibilities for women working on the margins. As Adrienne Rich wrote of feminist history, it "charges us, as women committed to the liberation of women, to know the past in order to consider what we want to conserve and what we want not to repeat or continue. . . . As differentiated from women's history, feminist history does not perpetuate the mainstream by simply invoking women to make the mainstream appear more inclusive" (1986, 146). This book intends to follow Rich, in that it is less concerned with the inclusion of women into a mainstream cinema tradition than it is with recognizing the marginality of these filmmakers' work and asking how such a location in the cultural field thwarted or generated artistic possibilities.

Unlike the literary realm, where women writers were able to enter with a consciousness of their situations and bring significant change to literary production itself, in the cinema, a medium dominated by industrial production for mass consumption, women were systematically excluded from creative roles until relatively recently. But while in the first half of the twentieth century in the Argentine cinema there is no Alfonsina Storni or Silvina Ocampo, the second half of the century saw the creative participation of Vlasta Lah, María Herminia Avellaneda, María Elena Walsh, Eva Landeck, Narcisa Hirsch, Lita Stantic, and María Luisa Bemberg. This book will pay close attention to little-known filmmakers and films in ways that, optimally, might renew the questions we ask of the role played by gender in the past and present of film production and viewing.

This book's account begins with the relatively abundant participation by women in Argentine film in the 1910s, then moves to the exclusion of women from creative roles in the cinema industry until the final crisis of the studios in the late 1950s. By this time an alternative film culture was flourishing in Argentina, marked by a profusion of *cineclubes* and specialized magazines and the opening of several film schools. In the 1960s the short film boomed, in large part as a product of new university-based filmmaking programs, but also encouraged by the state through funding and enabled by technological advances in film, cameras, sound, and other equipment. This convergence generated opportunities for nonindustrial film production that widened access to creative roles, and during the 1960s many women made short films using new production models that combined low costs, partial state funding or university support, and lack of commercial distribution (Listorti 299–300). The short format took on varied forms and objectives. While some filmmakers found in it an optimal medium for social critique and political militancy, others employed it as a means of aesthetic experimentation, while for still others it served as a stepping-stone toward features. Among those who went from directing short films to features in the 1970s and beyond are Landeck, Bemberg, and Lita Stantic.

Chapter 2 discusses three independently produced films directed by Landeck, revealing the challenges she encountered as a woman making films that engaged critically with the Argentine cultural and political field of her time. It examines how her feature films grapple with the social conflict and state violence of their time, as well as with the restrictive censorship inflicted on cultural production from the economic margins. Although *Gente en Buenos Aires* (1973) was made partly during the brief period of creative freedom often referred to as the *primavera camporista*, the effects of economic difficulties and state pressure are present both in its diegesis and in the story of its production and exhibition.[6] Under dictatorship, Landeck completed two more feature films independently of large production companies, on far lower budgets than for studio films. In *Ese loco amor loco* (1979), she employs censorship as a generative principle of the film's plot and alludes surprisingly, though indirectly, to the climate of fear and the society-wide submission to the repressive power of the state. She does so by creating a mystery whose resolution requires the spectator to consider the state violence that enforced its own unrepresentability. But, as Landeck recounts, each film was more compromised than the previous one—due to economic difficulties, competition for screens from large film producers, state censorship, and blacklisting—and she then left filmmaking in frustration (Trelles Plazaola 200–202).

Chapter 3 offers an account of feminism in film through the optic of the ideas of Simone de Beauvoir. The chapter begins with the brief directorial career of Vlasta Lah in the early 1960s, accounting for her films as early approximations to Beauvoir's ethics and, as such, early incursions of a modern feminist vision into the Argentine cultural field. Later, the long-term artistic collaboration of María Herminia Avellaneda and María Elena Walsh produced the film *Juguemos en el mundo* (1971), the first feature directed by a woman under the lengthy military dictatorship known as the Revolución Argentina. Avellaneda came to the cinema from television, where she had directed since the 1950s, and Walsh was already widely known as a singer-songwriter, poet, and playwright. Their self-funded collaboration parodies Argentine authoritarianism as retrograde and incompetent, yet permeating all aspects of society, from the public sphere to the domestic, but the film is particularly biting in its portrayal of the pressures of patriarchal authoritarianism on the lives of women at all levels of the social hierarchy.

The chapter closes with an account of two militant short films directed by Bemberg as part of her participation in feminist movements in Argentina in the 1970s. During the dictatorship, Bemberg began an extremely successful career, making six feature films between 1980 and 1993. Her case is unique, as she was a member of one of the wealthiest families in Argentina, self-financed her first film, *Momentos* (1980), and was able to find funding for subsequent productions due to its success. Her entry into direction was facilitated by Lita Stantic, with whom she collaborated to form a production company, GEA Cinematográfica (King 20–21). The attention lavished on Bemberg by audiences and critics is very well deserved, given her continuity as a director of quality, critical feature films that earned numerous international prizes, yet the consolidation of her status as a pioneering feminist director has cast a shadow over those women who preceded her in playing creative roles in the cinema.[7] In the words of Stantic, "The fact of setting out to direct films is already a very feminist action, because the cinema was always considered a man's job" (qtd. in Rangil 216). The filmmakers studied here all successfully met the challenge of making films.

Though many women have since directed, these successes do not mean that obstacles have been definitively overcome, especially in the production of the industry's larger-budget films, which very few women have directed. Clara Kriger points out that while women have opened spaces in production and opportunities have multiplied, a comparison of the percentage of women working with that of those trained to direct shows a continued disadvantage and a persistent celluloid ceiling (2014, n. pag.). Perhaps more immediately ominous, much state funding has recently been eliminated or redirected toward more corporate production, which does not bode well for the kind of independent production that has historically led to opportunities for women.[8]

1
A History of the Gendered Division of Labor in Argentine Cinema

To write a history of women in film production in twentieth-century Argentina is to tell of a shift from early collaborative, artisanal modes of production to an industrial mode characterized by a gendered division of labor, reinforced by union hierarchies, that excluded women from the so-called creative roles while limiting them to "feminized labor" (Hill 6–7), those lower-paid, repetitive tasks that corresponded to social constructions of domestic femininity: from the fine manual dexterity of sewing in the wardrobe department and cutting negatives, to the attention to detail of the "script girl" who ensured continuity from shot to shot.[1] Although solid information on the roles of women in both the early and studio periods in Argentina is still scarce, it appears safe to say that before the demise in the late 1950s of most of the large studios that produced the Argentine classical cinema, women had only participated somewhat regularly in the roles of producer and director during a brief period before the consolidation of the studios.[2]

The first feature-length films in Argentina were made in the 1910s, in an artisanal mode in which, the evidence suggests, production shared certain aspects with U.S. cinema of the time, which Shelley Stamp describes as "a flexible enterprise where it was relatively easy to move between creative positions and the role of 'director' as we now know it was less clearly defined" (5). While in Argentine cinema there is no equivalent of Lois Weber or Alice Guy Blaché—women who had creative control over a sustained production of films—the 1910s saw a relative abundance of women in creative roles when compared with subsequent decades.

Domingo Di Núbila mentions the foundation of the production company Platense Film by the actress "Camila Quiroga and her husband, Hector" (23), who hired accomplished directors and photographers from France to work in Argentina. The company later became Quiroga-Benoit Films and made the landmark feature *Juan sin ropa* in 1918.[3] Little research has been done on Camila Quiroga. During the same decade that Emilia Saleny directed the short *Paseo trágico* (1917) and the features *La niña del bosque* (1917), *Delfina* (1917), and *El pañuelo de Clarita* (1919), Elena Sansinena de Elizalde directed *Blanco y negro* (1919), and María B. de Celestini, *Mi derecho* (1920) (Mafud 2016; Fradinger 2014 ["Women in Argentine Silent Cinema"], n. pag.).[4] Moira Fradinger has uncovered a wealth of information on Saleny, generally considered the first woman to direct in Argentina. She founded an acting school, the Academia de Artes Cinematográficas, and in her films employed the child actors she trained. Her *El pañuelo de Clarita* is one of the few Argentine silent films to still exist today.[5] Recent archival research by Lucio Mafud adds information regarding the production of Saleny's films and uncovers other, even earlier, feature films, including *Un romance argentino* (also found under the title *El testamento*), produced by the philanthropic Comisión de Damas de la Asociación Hospital San Fernando (Ladies Commission of the San Fernando Hospital Association) and directed by its president Angélica García de García Mansilla in 1915, which would make it the first film directed by a woman and one of the very first Argentine feature-length films.[6]

Mafud finds revealing connections between the production of several of these early features and philanthropic associations: "It is no coincidence that the first women directors emerged from these philanthropic associations, since it is a space characterized by the central role of women of the elite sector" (2017, 53).[7] *Blanco y negro*, the central example discussed by Mafud, was produced by the Brigada de Señoras (Ladies' Brigade) of the Liga Patriótica Argentina (Argentine Patriotic League), to raise funds for the organization, which, "founded in January 1919, was established as a repressive organization on a national level with the purpose of combating any political and labor organizations that might threaten the economic status quo and the traditional hierarchies considered intrinsic components of its idea of the Nation. As such, its struggle was concentrated principally against anarchists, revolutionary syndicalism and any working-class tendencies sympathetic to the Russian Revolution, which it branded as foreign elements, alien to a supposed national order" (66–67). The Liga Patriótica played a notorious role in the violent repression of labor struggles and social protests, the most well-known of which are the Semana Trágica of 1919 and the 1920–1921 strikes on La Forestal, the British-owned company that exploited workers in slave-like conditions to cut much of the *quebracho* forests of Santa Fe and Chaco provinces in order to extract tannins (Cattaruzza 93–103).[8] While *Blanco y negro* was made under a preindustrial production model, such close links between economic power and film production have continued to condition the field of possibility of filmmaking throughout the ensuing hundred years, in terms of both representability and access to creative roles.

Although currently unavailable, the films of the 1910s studied by Mafud through press accounts beg further analysis, since around the time of the Centenario feminist activism was significant across the political spectrum. Meetings such as the Primer Congreso Femenino Internacional de la República Argentina—organized by the Asociación de Universitarias Argentinas in 1910—were held; more permanent organizations such as the Centro Feminista, the Liga Feminista Nacional, and the Primer Centro Feminista de Libre Pensamiento were founded, as were various publications in the interest of feminist issues and others aimed at a more general female readership, although these were often popular, escapist magazines (Lluch-Prats). Mafud writes of one film likely related to feminist activism, *Mi derecho*, possibly directed by María B.

de Celestini, which tells the story of a woman who bears a child out of wedlock and the efforts of her father to minimize the resulting scandal, which results in the separation of the child from the devastated mother and an eventual chance reunion (2016, 328).[9] According to Mafud, the film strays from the typical content of the films of the time. He writes that "it is important to point out that this thesis film that denounced social hypocrisy from the feminine point of view distances itself from the characteristic themes of the cinema of the period" (329–330). Mafud's account appears to locate the film as a parallel of the social problem films of the Progressive Era cinema of the United States.

This brief account of available evidence suggests that a variety of nonindustrial production models and a resulting wide field of creative possibilities for women existed in the 1910s. But since at present the films made by women during this period either no longer exist or are very difficult to view, and information available on the directors themselves is limited, I will move on to the sound cinema. First, however, I express hope that the films be made available by collectors or whoever might hold copies and that this intriguing moment—during which class, politics, and gender freely intersected on film before the eventual subsumption of the bulk of production under the aegis of the cinema industry—inspire further research.[10]

With the increasing professionalization of film production in Argentina, especially after the switch to sound cinema in the early 1930s, production and exhibition became far more capital-intensive. Money was invested on a much larger scale, studios were built, Taylorized production employing specialized technicians was implemented, national genres were developed, a star system came into being, unions were formed, a public was cultivated, and certain directors became established as reliable to entrust with the kind of capital it took to make, market, and screen a film. No women were among these.[11] While it is difficult at present to state unequivocally the causes of women's exclusion from film production, several recent studies of women's labor in early U.S. film find that a shift from a more artisanal production to a modern industry that divided labor into more clearly defined roles was decisive in women's exclusion (Mahar 179–208; Hill; Gaines 2018, 23–32), and based on the limited evidence available it appears that such an explanation holds true for Argentine cinema as well.[12] According to Mariana Inés Conde, the cinema studio workplace reflected the wider societal divisions of labor that limited the positions available to women: "Feminine labor, located in the context of the prevalent discourse on maternity as the natural social destiny of women, was necessarily, and from the beginning, impugned. Thus, as a product of the ties between maternity and the labor market, the idea of a maternity oriented toward society confirmed the occupations of teacher and nurse, as well as those of beneficence, which transformed gradually into social work" (2009, 164). The notion that women's place in the labor force corresponds to the privileged concept of maternity is reflected both in the roles traditionally open to women in the classical film industry workplace and in representations of women in the films produced by the same industry, to which I will return. As for the work open to women in the studios, while little solid information is available on the theme, a publicity film made in 1948 represents a clearly gendered division of labor.

The institutional documentary short *Cómo se hace una película argentina* (How an Argentine film is made) was produced in 1948 by various state institutions as part of a push by the Peronist state to boost the national film industry (Kriger 2009, 49–51). The film was directed by Arturo Mom and shown at the First Festival of Argentine Cinema in Mar del Plata. Several of the major studios collaborated, along with Laboratorios Alex and the main union of cinema workers of the time, Asociación Gremial de la Industria Cinematográfica Argentina, an industry-wide alliance of sectors that suggests that the film's representation of production faithfully reflects the prevalent practices of the time.

The film provides a behind-the-scenes account of studio filmmaking, documenting the various stages of production and depicting a wide variety of labor. Men occupy most of the positions, while, in addition to acting, women are shown as limited to several very specific tasks: sewing in the wardrobe department; applying makeup and hairdressing; and working as "negative cutters," the job of assembling the shots into a rough cut according to the continuity script and slate numbers. A few women are also seen on the set during filming; their specific roles are unclear, but they could well be continuity clerks—better known as "script girls"—charged with taking note of details to avoid continuity errors.

The film thus documents the gendered division of labor of the classical period of the Argentine studios, generally considered to be 1933 to 1956. Although a few women occasionally worked as scriptwriters and assistant directors, none directed films. The division, then, appears to correspond closely to that of the Hollywood studios, where women tended overwhelmingly to be limited to what are known as "below-the-line" professions. The term refers to a horizontal line that appears on production budget forms, above which are found creative costs (star actors, directors, writers, etc.), while below are the technical costs that include the labor of tradespeople and technicians (Banks 89). Women's place in both Hollywood and Argentine classical cinemas was, then, below the line. More specifically, in the Argentine studios, except for acting, women's participation was mostly limited to roles having to do with decoration, costumes, and a few tasks for which women were considered especially apt, such as that of *la script* (Hollywood's script girl) and *cortadora de negativo* (negative cutter), the latter described by Kristen Hatch as "tedious work that often fell to young working-class women" (n. pag.).[13] These few roles open to women represent a limitation to tasks considered traditionally feminine and associated with maternity, even as on a society-wide level women's workplace presence was expanding from the domestic to the public. While a few economically powerful women were able to work in the more creative role of producer, they were exceptions in an industrial cinema workplace characterized by a rigid hierarchy that was in part enforced by the unions, into which it was especially difficult for a woman to enter and where there was little prospect for advancement.[14]

The few published firsthand testimonies by women who worked in the industry support this account. Alicia Míguez Saavedra worked in various roles, beginning in 1938 on the script of Antonio Momplet's *Turbión*, and later became one of the few women to work as assistant director. The exceptional way she entered the industry is revealing of the lack of possibilities for women there. She recounted, "I was a big fan of the cinema, but as a spectator. I had never thought about being on the inside. Someone put me in contact with Estudios San Miguel for a translation that needed to be done quickly and that's how I got in. By chance" (Martín 12). Her first job in the industry came as the result of a mistake by Momplet, recently arrived from Spain, who, according to Míguez Saavedra, "thought I knew about cinema, about the technical side. But I had only done a translation here and there and wrote at the typewriter like I do now: with two fingers" (12). Despite her lack of experience, she managed to gain a foothold in the industry under the newly arrived director who was apparently ignorant of the de facto division of labor in the local production, and she kept working in film during a career that lasted five decades. When asked in 1983 if she had ever thought of directing, she replied diplomatically, "Yes, I thought that some day I'd be able to, but the fact of being busy with other things and that the cinema has changed so much (the milieu and the difficulties) made things turn out differently" (12). When asked in an earlier interview, in 1974, why there were so few women directors in the industry, Míguez Saavedra responded, "I suppose it's because the cinema is a relatively new industry and women are still struggling to break old molds," before mentioning Lah, Avellaneda, and Landeck as positive examples ("Los secretos del set" 14). Here Míguez Saavedra locates the problem in the stubborn structures whose persistence in the industrial cinema workplace had only recently begun to appear less monolithic.

Another illuminating story is that of Margarita Bróndolo, who had longed to work as an editor but had to settle for a career in the decidedly less creative role of negative cutter.[15] Born in 1911,

Bróndolo started working in the cinema in 1938 at the studio SIDE, and worked through the entire classical period and beyond, into the 1990s (E. López). Her entrance into the industry was facilitated by family connections. Her father began working in the 1930s at SIDE as a mechanic, and later her sister entered the studio as an accountant. Bróndolo had gone to sewing school, but when she first saw a soundstage, her interests changed. She recalled: "When I started to see what cinema was I forgot about the sewing machines and everything" (E. López). She inquired about work at the studio and was offered a job in accounting but refused, saying she wanted to work in production, on the set. The owner of SIDE, Alfredo Murúa, offered her a position in the film laboratory as negative cutter, which was reserved for women, and she accepted (E. López).

That the role of negative cutter was open to Bróndolo because she had attended sewing school confirms that the film industry was in no way free of wider societal biases based on gender. Bróndolo describes how, having become a friend of Vlasta Lah, who was then working as assistant director to her husband, Catrano Catrani, she had a brief opportunity to edit but was soon forced out due to her gender and had to return to cutting negatives (Soto n. pag.). She recounts that Lah "had written the script for a short and gave me the job of editing. She had a script girl and women in all sections. Vlasta went about making that short on her own account, she would film after finishing work, send the material to the laboratory and the next day I would clean the negative [then] she would send it off to copy. Since I was the editor, she would sit next to me at the Moviola and we would edit after hours. After all the guys would leave, I had permission to use a Moviola" (qtd. in Soto n. pag.). This nocturnal freedom would not last in the face of gender norms and union demands:

> But a big row broke out because the editor's assistants thought I wanted to take away their jobs, they didn't understand I was doing it for pleasure. What bothered them was to see me at the Moviola, because it turned out I knew more than the recent arrivals. . . . They didn't forgive me and started to scheme

against me. It was right at the time when the unions started to form. These guys went and protested: "If Margarita goes into editing we won't move up the ladder," and others chimed in, "Women can't be here, she needs to go back to cutting negative and stay there with the girls." They made such a scandal that the chief of the laboratory called me in . . . thinking I wanted to change section, and he asked me not to leave the negative in the hands of someone else. (qtd. in Soto n. pag.)

Bróndolo's defense, that she was only working in the capacity of editor on a single short made by a friend, outside of commercial channels, could not overcome the stubborn facticity of gender norms and union hierarchy. She was left lamenting the injustices faced by an ambitious woman in a male-dominated industry: "Later I confronted the guys for the whole sham they pulled by saying things that weren't true. Oh, I can tell you about the struggle of a woman to work in the cinema. It was tremendous. A hundred percent *machista*. . . . I had to leave the Moviola, very sadly, because so many got angry about it. I felt really bad about the injustice of the situation. Some day I'll be able to, I consoled myself, but it wasn't to be. . . . Officially I was never able to edit" (qtd. in Soto). While it is difficult to know how typical Bróndolo's story is, simply because data do not exist and few interviews with women in the industry were published, she tells of a deep personal disillusionment brought about by the stubbornly gendered division of labor existing within the midcentury industry.[16] The question of what enforced this division is difficult to answer conclusively, but it seems safe to assume that the union hierarchy in combination with the lack of film schools prevented women from entering roles reserved for men. Bróndolo references the latter in an interview in which she looks back at the studio period: "Before, we had to learn from each other because there were no film schools, nothing, no books. So we had to always be alert, to catch whatever was said so we could take advantage of it to expand our knowledge" (E. López). Without the opportunities that would later be provided by film schools, the only route to advance in the industry was through the ranks, yet there mobility was blocked by established professionals disinclined to tolerate competition from women. Looking back, Bróndolo acknowledges that things had since changed for women: "I wanted to edit for many years. . . . But no, at that time the terrible machismo didn't let me. Later, when some young women tried to edit, I told them to not let what happened to me happen to them, because now things are different. So fight. At that time I couldn't because it would have meant fighting against a wall" (E. López). While Bróndolo was unable to overcome the rigid hierarchy she describes, Lah was able to do so temporarily and, in part, it seems, through personal connections. She worked as assistant director on about twenty films, many directed by her husband, Catrano Catrani, before directing *Las furias* (1960) and *Las modelos* (1963) on the margins of the moribund industry, thus becoming the first woman in four decades to direct a feature-length film in Argentina. Lah's work is discussed in detail in chapter 3.[17]

From the 1930s to the 1950s, film production was dominated by the commercial studios, but short films were made under other modes of production, in which women such as Amanda Lucía Turquetto and Irena Dodal were occasionally able to direct. Turquetto worked in an institutional mode of production, for the Instituto Cinematográfico del Estado (ICE; State Cinematographic Institute), a division of the Ministerio de Justicia e Instrucción Pública (Ministry of Justice and Public Education), which made short films exalting touristic sites that were shown as complements to regular features in commercial cinemas. The ICE—earlier the Instituto Cinematográfico Argentino—was headed by Carlos Alberto Pessano, the conservative nationalist journalist and, since 1932, director of *Cinegraf*, a luxurious magazine to which he contributed a monthly editorial that, as Raúl Horacio Campodónico writes, "systematically referred to the local cinema through guidelines as exacerbatedly normative as they were moralizing" (59). The ICE had been proposed as early as 1936 by Pessano on the pages of *Cinegraf* as an "organism that would institute a comptroller adequate to the psychology and the problems of this People, so that viewers would know, at least, what will be shown to them on screen and thus be defended against deceptive propagandas and subterfuges" (qtd. in Campodónico 60). Pessano's censorious attitude toward the cinema reflected that of many nations in the 1930s, apprehensive about the medium's effects on a mass public it considered vulnerable to suggestion and prone to irrational behavior. The 1938 measure that created ICE was inspired by an official trip taken by the senator Matías G. Sánchez Sorondo to fascist Italy and Germany, where he admired the strong control exerted by the state over cultural production, and the cinema in particular, under Mussolini and Hitler (63–68). This propagandistic vision of the cinema drove Sánchez Sorondo's proposal for the law: "It is necessary . . . to consider if—art or industry or industrial art—the cinematographic spectacle is simple entertainment, trivial enjoyment, or the most accessible, attractive and powerful of the media at the disposal of the humanity of our time to transmit an idea" (qtd. in Campodónico 72). Sánchez Sorondo's belief was clearly the latter, and his consideration of the cinema as an instrument of propaganda responds to a fear, typical of the time, of a confluence of modern mass communications, revolutionary ideals, and the working class.

In addition to exercising certain legal controls over film production more generally, ICE produced at least five films between 1941 and 1943, when its production was halted due to the shortage of film stock brought about by the war and its subsequent closure by decree at the end of that year. The stated purpose of these films was in line with the mission of ICE as it appears in a text at the end of *Playa Grande* (1943): "acercar a los argentinos al major conocimiento de su patria y de mostrar a los extranjeros algunos aspectos de una gran nación en marcha" (to bring to Argentines a greater knowledge of their country and show foreigners several aspects of a great nation on the march). With such specific objectives and limited production, ICE was apparently free of the hierarchies that determined much of the commercial industry's division of labor, and, based on the very limited evidence available, there was a greater degree of opportunity for women in creative roles.

Playa Grande (1943) was directed, according to its title sequence, by Amanda Lucía and Hector Bernabó. Angela López Ruiz provides the codirector's full name as Amanda Lucía Turquetto and describes *Playa Grande* as "an artistic exercise in non-narrative filmmaking... characterized by radiant framing and shots filled with isolated details set to minimalist music. It is a highly visual documentary, with geometric compositions and a radical approach to montage that brings together long, slow takes and extreme close-ups of sand, skin, and nets to tell the story of a day at the beach in Argentina" (244). Although accurate, this description does not consider the film as a product of an institution "a cargo de Carlos Alberto Pessano" (directed by Carlos Alberto Pessano), as the film's opening titles state. While the film does tell the story of a day at the beach, its aesthetic responds as much to the institutional imperatives described by Pessano and Sánchez Sorondo as to "artistic" concerns. The film's melding of modernist aesthetics and touristic publicity elides completely (and predictably, given the presence of Pessano as executive producer) any less-than-ideal aspects of Argentina. In it, as Clara Kriger notes, "the particularity is that in every case its inhabitants had a notably European appearance" (2010, 274). The classical beauty of the abundant women of northern European features seen in the film recalls the late-1930s work of Leni Riefenstahl, such as *Olympia* (1938). Achieving such aesthetic purity is, of course, no great feat, beyond the choices of location filming at a beach resort unfrequented by society's have-nots and a casting on the basis of race. A telluric correspondence between the seascape and the women who inhabit it is articulated formally through a shot-countershot dynamic that links the beauty of the European faces and bodies with that of the inviting sea and untrodden dunes, before moving on to an interlude of folkloric imagery of traditional fishermen attending to their picturesque labors. Little information on Amanda Lucía Turquetto is available, and the film prompts more questions about her as a director than it answers. The objectives shared by the ICE films are clearly passed down from their institutional producer, so while *Playa Grande* is undeniably beautifully shot and edited, its aesthetic is in the service of the nationalistic insecurities and touristic priorities of ideologues like Pessano.

In a less institutional mode of production, Irena Dodal made short films on dance and folkloric themes in the 1950s and 1960s. Born Irena Rosnerová in 1900 in Czechoslovakia, she there produced animated films with her husband, Karel Dodal, in the 1930s for institutional and advertising clients (Strusková 86, 163–165, 197–209). In 1936 the couple made the animated *Adventures of a Ubiquitous Fellow*, which they would later rework in Argentina as *La reina de las ondas*. In 1938 Karel Dodal left for the United States, while Irena remained behind in Czechoslovakia, planning to soon follow him. But Germany soon occupied the country, and, as a Jew, she was unable to get approval to travel. On June 20, 1942, she was interned in the Theresienstadt Ghetto, and in the fall of that year she became part of a crew organized by the Nazis to make a propaganda film depicting the ghetto as a model resettlement community for Jews. In February 1945 she was transported, along with 1,200 other persons, to Switzerland and soon after traveled to join her husband in the United States, where the couple tried to continue to make a living from animated film production. They ran into difficulties due to a lack of demand, and when, in 1948, they were offered a two-year contract to produce films by the Argentine minister of education, Oscar Ivanissevich, they accepted and moved to Buenos Aires.

In Argentina the Dodals set up a studio, Argencolor, and made several films, including *La reina de las ondas* (1947), a fourteen-minute animated short produced by the Ministry of Education that reproduces the original *Adventures of a Ubiquitous Fellow* with some deletions and new footage. In it, a childlike extraterrestrial comes to earth, landing in a futuristic city, and soon meets *la reina de las ondas* (the queen of the radio waves), a ghostlike woman who teaches him about the workings of radio transmission. At one point, when asked to show the invisible radio waves, the queen resorts to visual metaphor through the use of her "micro-cine," in which the two watch a nonanimated film that shows waves breaking on a beach, undulations of grain swaying in the wind, and ripples caused by rocks thrown into a lake. After Argencolor closed in the early 1950s, Irena Dodal turned to documentaries of dance performance and folklore, making *Apollon Musagete* (1951), *Don Juan de Zarissa* (1956), *Dos danzas contemporáneas* (1956), *La suite Argentina* (1956), and *La tierra canta* (1965) (Strusková 322). She was also active in the theater, teaching acting and directing plays.[18]

The sixteen-minute *Apollon Musagète* was made in 1951 and there are mentions of it being shown at festivals in 1952.[19] It was filmed in Studios Emelco, produced by well-known arts patron Marcelo De Ridder, and represents a performance of the title ballet with music by Igor Stravinsky and choreography by George Balanchine, danced by members of the company of the Teatro Colón, with Victor Ferrari and the famous María Ruanova. In a very midcentury modernist mise-en-scène, the lighting renders the background abstract, and a sophisticated decoupage includes superimpositions in which dancers from two separate shots are coordinated, emphasizing the bodies of the dancers in movement. Dodal's other films do not appear to be available. According to Eva Strusková, she passed away in Buenos Aires in 1989 (332).

Though there may be others still undiscovered, these two women who directed beyond the margins of the industry are exceptional during the period that runs from the 1920s through the late 1950s, when the studios that had for decades enforced a near-total absence of women in creative roles in the cinema entered into crisis. Shaken by the elimination of the generous state subsidies they had received under Peronism, the studios drastically lowered their production and were forced into competition with more independent productions. An alternative film culture had begun to appear around 1950, spurred on by a profusion of *cineclubes*—where cinephile members paid for long-term membership that granted them access to screenings—specialized magazines, and the opening of several film schools.[20] As Félix-Didier writes, the renewal of the field "did not originate in the industry, but rather in the world of the cine-clubs and the vocational workshops that had begun to operate a few years before, which allowed the young generations to gain familiarity with cinema history and practice" (2003 ["Introduction"], 12). While the renewal known as the Nuevo Cine is generally associated with the feature-length films of the decade that began in 1960, its presence is evident in the area of short filmmaking by the mid-1950s, and it was underway several years earlier in the *cineclubes*.

José Martínez Suárez, who began a long career in the industry in the 1940s before directing more independently from the 1960s on, attributes the rise of the *cineclub* in part to state intervention under Perón: "The *cineclub* had a great moment during the Peronist government, when a very strange thing happened, since they prohibited films. Nevertheless, they let the *cineclubes* show them, and that was when people rushed to the Cine-Club Núcleo, selling out the theater" (Valles 114). In addition to the *cineclubes*' effect of increasing the sophistication of viewers by programming less commercial cinema, they provided a node around which a community of cinephile filmmakers could form and a venue for the viewing of the short films they would soon make, as Martínez Suárez recounts of the aptly named Núcleo: "We have to . . . point out the readiness that el Negro [Salvador Sammaritano, organizer of the Núcleo] always had to show Argentine shorts: he turned to short filmmakers because he realized they were the gateway to the feature film. If we take a look at the names of the excellent directors we had and continue to have in Argentina, we'll see that all come from the short film" (Valles 116). As its hand-typed programs attest, the Núcleo was one of the first venues to show foundational shorts like Fernando Birri's *Tire dié* (in 1958) and David José Kohon's *Buenos Aires* (in 1959) (Cine club Núcleo 1958, 1959). On the side of production, the use of more mobile and cheaper equipment—especially 16-millimeter film, lightweight recorders that made it possible to capture direct sound on location, and the zoom lens—was opening documentary and short filmmaking to new filmmakers and subjects all over the world, and its impact was felt in Argentina as well.

These new models of exhibition and production led to many short films being made through a combination of partial state funding or institutional support, low costs, and alternative distribution. Citing Simón Feldman, one of the original participants in the movement, Javier Cossalter puts the number of shorts made from 1958 to 1965 at nearly 300 (2015, 313). In addition to the quantity of films, it is important to attend to the wide variety of objectives of the participant filmmakers. Many cultivated the format as a means by which to eventually progress to the feature film, but due to its mobility and low cost, it also lent itself very well to socially engaged and militant cinema, documentary shorts, and aesthetic experimentation.

Several filmmakers studied in Europe and returned to Argentina, among them Fernando Birri, Simón Feldman, and Mabel Itzcovich. Born in Rosario in 1927, Itzcovich became an important early force in independent filmmaking. After studies at the Institut des hautes études cinématographiques (IDHEC) in Paris in the early 1950s, she returned to Argentina. There she worked extensively as a film critic, and with Feldman, her husband, founded the Seminario de Cine, which provided instruction modeled on the training they received in Paris, and the journal *Cuadernos de Cine*, in which they argued to legitimize the short film and the 16-millimeter format. They did so in the interest of filmmaking and viewing freed from the limitations and exclusions that characterized the studio model, a project that would bear fruit with a boom in the short film format and, eventually, with the feature-length films of the Generación del 60 (Sammaritano 1962 ["Diccionario de la nueva generación argentina: Segunda parte"], 10; Félix-Didier 2003 ["La crítica de cine en los 60"], 329).

In 1961, Itzcovich described the new cinema of that moment as marked by "a desire for authenticity that results in a delving into our surrounding reality in order to understand characters, idioms, language, places and lifestyles identified with our psychological or social reality" ("Hora cero" 9). In her description of the new cinema's sustained attention to the national reality, Itzcovich mentions its exploration of a psychological reality that she would go on to explore in her own shorts *De los abandonados* (1962) and *Soy de aquí* (1965). In these, she dramatizes encounters between historical events and individual subjectivities and the heightened political consciousness that results. The fact that the subjectivities in question are those of women is no minor detail. These take the form of voiceover narrations that perturb the usual authoritative male voiceover by recognizing a lack of knowledge and a desire for it. These female character-narrators are locatable in terms of social class, and though unseen, are present in the diegesis, taking part in the events documented as perceptive witnesses. In the 10-minute *De los abandonados*, the narrator is a middle-class woman who inquires, investigates, and learns. In *Soy de aquí* the young woman of the working class who narrates has no such luxury to inquire and investigate, but when events involve her, she perceptively draws conclusions about the relationship between her social class and national politics.

De los abandonados explores the condition known as "hospitalism," which results from the separation of infants from their mother when hospitalized, and endorses a new model of care in which the mother can accompany her child during the stay. Hospitalism became an important subject of Argentine pediatric medicine in the 1960s, when the ideas of emotional bonding and maternal deprivation developed by the British psychologist John Bowlby were taken up locally, most notably in publications and practices by Florencio Escardó and Eva Giberti (Diamant).

The film opens by documenting the public Hospital de Niños Ricardo Gutiérrez in Buenos Aires. Its waiting room is crowded with mothers who are clearly not well off. The female voiceover in the first person establishes an inquiring presence:

> Cada mañana alguien, entre muchos, llega al Hospital de Niños. Yo también estoy aquí, y veo. ¿El motivo? Mi motivo no importa ahora. Veo lo niños. Sus ojos interrogan y sus voces no necesitan hablar. Gritan. Los escucho y siento su soledad. La impotencia del sufrimiento. En un lugar así parece natural hablar de ellos, de los abandonados."

> Each morning someone, among many, arrives to the Children's Hospital. I'm also here, and I see. The reason? My reasons aren't important now. I see the children. Their eyes implore and their

voices do not need to speak. They cry. I hear them and feel their solitude. The powerlessness of their suffering. In such a place it seems natural to speak of them, of the abandoned ones.

The title card appears as the final words are pronounced. The observer, voiced in Norma Aleandro's middle-class register, sets out to discover how these mothers live and how they interact with a state institution. She is shown photos of the mothers' neighborhood, which is her initial experience of a *villa miseria* (shantytown). Then, when she visits the home of one of the mothers she had met in the hospital, one of the photos becomes a moving picture. The narrator is invited into the modest home, and the camera enters with her, filming the impoverished interior. She experiences an epiphany: "Fue entonces que entendí. Estaba hablando de la madre, pero también del hijo. No podía separarlos. ¿Qué pasa cuando este vínculo se corta?" (Then I understood. I was speaking of the mother, but also of the child. I couldn't separate them. What happens when this connection is broken?).

To answer her own question she returns to the Children's Hospital, which takes on new meaning as she empathizes with the child's alienation, becoming a place "de ventanas clausuradas, de interminables corredores, de juegos silenciosos y vacíos" (of closed windows, interminable corridors, empty and silent games). The imagery expresses this alienation with extended takes of abandoned and neglected institutional spaces that immerse the viewer in the silent emptiness and cold institutional logic the children are forced to negotiate on their own, deprived of the support of their mother. The narrator further explains her need for knowledge: "Necesitaba saber qúe pasa cuando el niño enfermo, vulnerable, era separado día y noche, semanas o meses de la madre" (I needed to know what happens when the sick, vulnerable child was separated day and night, for weeks or months, from its mother). Images of the interior of the children's wards provide an answer, showing the suffering evident on the faces of the children, as the voiceover describes what she observes and then draws conclusions: "Primero la rebelión, el llanto. ¿Pero cuánto puede durar la rebelión y el llanto? Duran exactamente el tiempo que tarda en llegar la indiferencia y el rechazo" (First rebellion, then weeping. But how long can rebellion and weeping last? They last exactly the time it takes to get to indifference and rejection).

The symptoms seen by viewer and narrator are those of hospitalism, a condition the narrator describes as "una profunda perturbación psíquica . . . consecuencia del brutal aislamiento. . . . El niño alejado de la madre ha roto sus vínculos, su proceso de integración a la comunidad humana" (a deep psychic perturbation . . . consequence of brutal isolation. . . . The child distanced from the mother has broken its links, its process of integration into the human community). The film concludes with the documentation of a solution, a new practice, introduced in the experimental Sala 17 (Ward 17) of the Hospital de Niños by Escardó and Giberti, in which mother and child can remain together during the hospitalization. This practice is integral to Escardó's philosophy of "la nueva pediatría" (new pediatrics) in which, as he wrote, "if the child forms a structural part of the mother-child binomial, as we have always known to be true, in the new pediatrics it is only reasonable to treat the functioning binomial" (qtd. in Wasertreguer and Waizman 37). Revolutionary at the time, the practice faced strong resistance but continued to be used (38–43).

In Itzcovich's second film, *Soy de aquí*, the political consciousness of a sample of the Peronist working class in the context of the prohibition of Peronism is observed, inflected by the consciousness of a young working-class woman. The film formulates two stories—one personal, one collective—and postulates their inseparability. One tells of the formation of the political conscience of the young woman, while the other, more static, describes the context in which this happens: the neighborhood of Sarandí, beyond the southern limit of the capital, among its politically disenchanted working-class inhabitants. The 15-minute film opens with the voiceover of the young woman, retrospective as it opens the film: "Ahora se lo ve tranquilo, olvidado. ¿Quién piensa en Sarandí?" (Now it looks calm, forgotten. Who thinks about Sarandí?). She speaks from a future position of an already raised political conscience, one capable of considering the local from an exterior perspective—"¿Quién piensa en estos barrios?" (Who thinks about these neighborhoods?)—before beginning a narration of the past decades: "Pero mi barrio tiene una historia . . ." (But my neighborhood has a story . . .).

From a Peronist family, she recounts childhood memories of the general's overthrow, the short-lived hope of the Frondizi presidency when Peronism was briefly legalized, the election of the Peronist resistance leader Andrés Framini as governor of Buenos Aires province, the subsequent annulment of his election, and the military rebellions of the "Azules y Colorados" (Blues and Reds). The latter, of prime importance for what is to come in the film, was a dispute in 1962 and 1963 between two sectors of the armed forces opposed in their strategy for dealing with the stubborn fact of the Peronist movement, which persisted despite its proscription and was able to disrupt the political system that tried to ban it even in the physical absence of its leader.

The focalization then shifts to a group of young men from working-class families. Each takes a brief turn providing a voice-over, giving his age—all are children of the Peronist period, born between 1944 and 1947—and employment, then all are seen and heard in conversations. These reveal that while their parents might have been part of the Peronist resistance in the years that followed the coup of 1955, in the absence of Peronism from official politics these young men grew up as part of "una clase obrera fiel a una identidad política pero sin partido" (Sigal 199) and as such are politically alienated and anomic. Immediately following the conversation between the young men, seven brief shots show local women, some idling in doorways, other carrying out domestic tasks. None speak. Interpretation of this contrast—speaking men, silent women—is left up to the viewer, but the disparity between the more gregariously wandering men and the mostly house-bound women could not be clearer.

The film then follows the group of young men on a night out dancing, then a day of idling, during which one member, Enrique, a volunteer firefighter and boyfriend of the narrator, is suddenly called to a fire. Here the film tells, through documentary footage and reports heard on a diegetic radio, of the events surrounding the historic fire of August 11, 1962, that destroyed the SEGBA power plant in Dock Sud, leaving sections of Buenos Aires without power for up to a month. The fire's origin and its spread were attributed to the conflict between military factions, and the radio reports an episode in which a military unit blocking the Avellaneda Bridge attacked a fire truck that tried to cross the bridge to get to the fire, killing a firefighter. The narrative focalization then returns to the original young woman, who is worried that her boyfriend might have been the one killed. Although it then turns out that the victim is a different man, the woman's voiceover explains how the episode has raised her consciousness and politicized her, making her think beyond the confines of Sarandí to how wider-scale politics have local consequences. Although her boyfriend attributes the other man's death to bad luck, she brings greater insight:

> Había un bombero muerto. Para Enrique no había pasado nada, nada más que una desgracia. Para Enrique y tal vez para muchos otros. Pero yo entonces supe que el barrio no termina en el club, en Mitre, en el terraplén o en la laguna. Entonces lo vi diferente al barrio. Entonces supe que el barrio tenía una historia.
>
> There was a dead fireman. According to Enrique, nothing had happened, just bad luck. According to Enrique and perhaps many others. But I realized then that the neighborhood doesn't end at the club, at Mitre Avenue, at the embankment or the lagoon. I began to see the neighborhood in a different way. I found out that the neighborhood had a history.

With this realization by its narrator, *Soy de aquí* completes its powerful account of a woman reaching a political consciousness in the face of working-class anomie in Perón's absence, the kind of consciousness that would expand across society in the second half of the decade, in part due to filmmakers' efforts to represent places and perspectives that had previously been invisible in the national culture, closing the breach between the left intelligentsia and nationalist mass politics.

In the short films made by Itzcovich a new political subject is born: a politically aware woman, ready to participate actively in social change. Though both nationally and personally this concientization would turn tragic with the brutal and arbitrary violence of the military dictatorship, it persists in the widespread movements that today resist the neoliberal project. Itzcovich stayed active in film (directing the short *Los caras sucias* in 1969) and journalism, but after the kidnapping and disappearance of her highschool aged daughter, Laura, at the hands of the dictatorship, she went into exile in Rome. Upon her return to Argentina in 1984, she stayed very active in journalism and cultural criticism until her death in 2004.

In addition to the educational possibilities in Europe, the local film schools also provided opportunities for women, and many directed. There were several schools, but two of the earliest and most important were the Instituto de Cinematografía of the Universidad Nacional del Litoral, also known as the Escuela Documental de Santa Fe, and the Escuela de Cine de la Universidad de La Plata. The Escuela Documental, opened in 1956, was modeled on Rome's Centro Sperimentale, where its founder, Fernando Birri, had studied. Birri is often referred to as the father of the Nuevo Cine Latinoamericano and the films made under his auspices generally denounced social injustice from the political left without necessarily engaging with gender issues. Judging by titles and synopses, the shorts directed by women in the context of the Escuela Documental do not appear to be exceptions to this pattern.[21] Nelly Borroni directed *El puente de papel* (1962); Heredia Marino made *Feria franca* (1961); Elena de Azcuénaga codirected *La inundación en Santa Fe* (with Juan Oliva and Edgardo Pallero, 1959) and directed *Quinto dedo varo* (1959), *Luxación congénita de cadera* (1960), and *Opera el profesor Clarence Crafford* (1960) (Birri 126–128); Marilyn Contardi made *Jardín de infantes* (1964) and *La vieja ciudad* (1969) (Truglio 313; Gigena n. pag.); and Dolly Pussi,

El hambre oculta (1965), *Pescadores* (1968), and *Operativo Brigadier Estanislao López* (1973).[22]

At the time of writing, to my knowledge only Pussi's films are available.[23] The twelve-minute *El hambre oculta*, a collaboration with the United Nations campaign against world hunger, formulates one of the decade's most powerful denunciations of social injustice. Filmed in part in the *villas miseria* near Santa Fe, it documents the malnutrition suffered by local marginalized children before expanding its scope to other areas of Latin America, Asia, and Africa.[24] This allows the film to attribute malnutrition to a faulty distribution of resources and thus gesture toward larger-scale revolutionary solutions that might reconfigure both international and national economic relations, like those soon taken up by films like *La hora de los hornos*.

Pescadores, at twenty-six minutes, limits its denunciation to a local scope, documenting the conditions of fishermen in the area of Santa Fe and their exploitation at the hands of the brokers who buy their product and sell it on to market. The film combines footage of fishermen working on the Paraná River near Santa Fe with interviews with fishermen, brokers, and experts, supplemented by music composed and performed by Daniel Viglietti, the well-known Uruguayan singer-songwriter. He wrote the lyrics, which reference the plight of the fishermen, after listening to the interviews. The combination of these materials produces frequent vertical montage effects that mediate the testimonies, confirming some and casting doubt on others. The latter happens in the case of the fish broker, who, it is suggested through images of the fishermen's backbreaking labor with premodern means, profits undeservedly from the efforts and suffering of others. As images are seen of fishing and a precarious domesticity, complaints heard from a fisherman round out the film's message: the broker monopolizes the market and exploits the fishermen's labor. The film's central point is further authorized by the words of the expert, the "Director Nacional de Limnología" (national director of limnology) (Truglio 314), who argues that despite their great potential, the local fisheries produce relatively little, and thus better development of the industry through modernization of the equipment used by the fishermen is needed. Yet despite a need for action on a scale beyond the capacity of the fishermen, the state remains absent.

Operativo Brigadier Estanislao López (1973) is the product of a specific perspective during a unique moment in Argentine history, the brief period of high optimism on the Peronist revolutionary left during the Cámpora presidency. Its twenty-three minutes document an operation undertaken by members of the Juventud Peronista in the province of Santa Fe, in which young volunteers worked on improvement projects in *villas miseria* and poor rural areas, some of which were formerly administered by the infamous British company La Forestal. An extended discourse by a young Juventud Peronista leader, Jorge Obeid, lays out the meaning of the operation for revolutionary Peronism:

> Las tareas de reconstrucción nacional . . . tienen un significado esencialmente político. Significan organizar y movilizar a nuestro pueblo en pos de conseguir sus objetivos revolucionarios que se ha fijado hace ya muchos años y de estar alerta para resistir a cualquier embate que desde la oligarquía, desde el imperialismo o de cualquiera de los agentes del continuismo que aún está presente incluso en el seno de nuestro movimiento y de nuestro gobierno popular puedan querer dar el zarpazo contra ese gobierno.[25]

> The tasks of national reconstruction . . . have an essentially political meaning. They signify the organization and mobilization of our *pueblo* in pursuit of its revolutionary objectives that were set many years ago and their readiness to resist any attack by the oligarchy, by imperialism or by any of the agents of continuism that, still present even in the heart of our movement and our popular government, might attempt to deal a blow against that government.

The optimism expressed by Obeid was very short-lived, and Pussi's career in film would soon be suspended under the dictatorship.[26] But since the early 1980s she has worked extensively in production with Bemberg, Stantic, and many others, and in 1990 she directed *Sabemos mirar*, a twenty-five-minute documentary produced mostly with funding from British, Spanish, and Australian television, on the role of rock music under the dictatorship. She currently directs the Escuela de Cine Documental at the Universidad de San Martín, in Buenos Aires province (Ciucci).

The Escuela Documental de Santa Fe was closed as the 1976 coup approached, and most of its films were lost or burned during the dictatorship (Truglio 315–316). While it was perhaps the most important film school in terms of socially engaged filmmaking, it was not the only educational institution to produce such work. The Escuela de Cine de la Universidad Nacional de La Plata began to teach film production in 1955 and later employed many filmmakers of the Generación del 60 as faculty members. The reputation of the program in the 1960s was that of training filmmakers with an orientation toward narrative, even commercial production, though toward the end of the decade this emphasis produced a forceful reaction from within the program and a move toward a more politically engaged cinema, in which Silvia Verga played an important role.[27]

Verga has since been referred to more often by her married name, Silvia Oroz, under which she has become a highly published scholar of Latin American film and a professor in universities in Argentina, Brazil, and elsewhere (Di Cola 209). As a student she directed the five-minute *Mayo* (1970) and the eight-minute *Bienamémonos* (1971) (Peña 2006) and formed part of a class that in 1967 had filmed short exercises on the theme of taxis. Several of these indulge in formal experimentation derivative of some of the early, self-reflexive films of Jean-Luc Godard, an influence the filmmakers would renounce three years later when, in the context of heightened political engagement in the wake of the Cordobazo, they added retrospective commentaries and supplementary footage and edited the shorts together to form the twenty-seven-minute *Los taxis* (1970). Many of the commentaries and added footage reflect the filmmakers' own processes of politicization in the three-year interval between the exercises and the final version, during which *La hora de los hornos* had shaken the field of politically engaged filmmaking. The resulting film contains critical reflections from a position of heightened consciousness on the earlier films' more formalist concerns, the directors' own lack of political sophistication at the time, and especially the pedagogical practice of the film school at La Plata. Verga directed one episode, in which her voice-over reflections resonate with the critique by Solanas and Getino of second cinema:

> Hace cinco años que estoy en la escuela de cine. Son cinco años que me muevo entre los mitos políticos y estéticos. Son cinco años que trato de asimilar lo concreto de esos mitos creados por debilidad política, falta de conocimiento y una pseudo-posición de avanzada. El cine elegido no será en colores, ni en 35 milímetros, tampoco será distribuido por la Metro-Goldwyn-Mayer o cualquiera de sus similares, porque la elección es un cine con forma de lucha.
>
> I've been in film school for five years. For five years I've moved among political and aesthetic myths. For five years I've tried to assimilate the particulars of those myths created by political weakness, lack of knowledge and a pseudo-avant-garde stance. The chosen cinema will not be in color, nor in 35 millimeter, nor will it be distributed by Metro-Goldwyn-Mayer or any of its equivalents, because the choice is for a cinema in the form of struggle.

In the militant terms of the time, Verga's commentary is a clear rejection of what she and the others saw as a faulty orientation of the film program at La Plata toward production values, the market, and the type of auteur aesthetic that Solanas and Getino rejected as bourgeois second cinema. The resulting imperative rejects training for the workplace in favor of a conceptual radicalization of the instruction.

Verga was also among the six codirectors of the militant feature-length *Informes y testimonios: La tortura política en argentina, 1966–1972* (1973), released during the Cámpora presidency, which both documents and re-creates scenes of state violence under the long dictatorship that began in 1966 under Juan Carlos Onganía (Massari 27). The disturbing footage includes re-creations, based on oral testimony by victims, of kidnapping and torture carried out by police and paramilitary forces. These are filmed in distanced long takes that alternate with fixed-camera shots showing the sites of the corruption and state violence described in testimony by various individual voice-overs. The film also examines the theme of the *villa miseria* through documentary footage and the voice-over of a villa inhabitant who attributes its existence to uneven development produced by capitalism as a result of its need for centers of industrial production in close proximity to sources of cheap labor pools: "Somos la mano be obra barata que permite a los empresarios acumular grandes ganancias" (We are the cheap labor that permits businessmen to accumulate huge profits). Later, several of the makers of *Informes y testimonios* worked on the faculty of the film program at the Universidad Nacional de La Plata, but after intense politicization and growth, especially around the time of the Cámpora presidency, the film program was closed by the dictatorship in 1976 (Truglio 322).

Another institution that trained filmmakers is the Asociación de Cine Experimental (ACE), founded in 1956 (Getino 44). Lita Stantic, who began studying there in 1963, describes it as "a house in Pompeya run by the students" (Eseverri and Peña 84).[28] Another student at the ACE was Eva Landeck, who studied there for four years, then made the short films *Barrios y teatros de Buenos Aires* (1963), *Domingos en Hyde Park* (1965), *Las ruinas de Pompeya* (1963), *Entremés* (1966), *Horas extras* (1967), and *El empleo* (1970) (Trelles Plazaola 197), before going on to direct three features in the 1970s. Landeck's career and films are discussed in chapter 2 of this book.

Other organizations played important roles in stimulating the production of short films, among them the Centro Experimental de Realización Cinematográfica (CERC), the Asociación de Realizadores de Cortometraje, the Instituto Torcuato Di Tella, and the Fondo Nacional de las Artes (FNA; National Fund for the

Arts), a state institution founded in 1958. Beginning in 1962, the FNA created opportunities for previously inexperienced filmmakers by producing short films on, as its catalog states, "the disciplines that the FNA protects, that is, visual arts, music, literature, theater, cinema, folklore," through "support in the form of credit that can amount to one hundred percent of the production budget" (Fondo Nacional de las Artes n.d., 7). The films, limited to a duration of between five and twenty minutes, would be produced and acquired by the FNA, which would act as distributor. The program enabled the creation of a variety of works by filmmakers who otherwise would not likely have had access to the medium. As Cossalter writes, the FNA "was one of the institutions that most supported the innovative short film between the late 1950s and the mid-sixties, promoting works with new themes and a marked aesthetic experimentation" (2017, 9).

The most well-known FNA films are those coproduced by the Universidad de Tucumán and directed by Jorge Prelorán, who worked with his wife, Mabel Prelorán, and Ana Montes. The latter, an ethnographer, after working in production in the 1960s with Raymundo Gleyzer and Prelorán, filmed ethnographic documentary footage on her own and eventually codirected a work of visual anthropology with Anne Chapman, *Los Onas: Vida y muerte en Tierra del Fuego*, in 1977. Campo describes the purpose of the film as to "preserve the thought of the last Ona woman, her vision on contemporary society and the customs of her ancestors" (89). According to her daughter, even in this marginal mode of production Montes faced difficulties due to her gender. She often worked with her husband, an archaeologist, of whom Montes's daughter says, "At that time my father was tremendously *machista*. And she held herself back, preventing herself from breaking barriers out of ideological conviction" (Santoro n. pag.).

The FNA program opened many possibilities in the area of documentary shorts on artists and folklore, and several women directed. Perla Lich (Lichtenstein) codirected, with Jaime Graschinsky, *Antonio Pujía,* a nine-minute "documentary film on art, that intends to . . . translate into filmic images the works and ideas of an important Italian sculptor who lives in Argentina" (Fondo Nacional de las Artes 1973, 2). Lichtenstein later went on to work as production manager on films by Carlos Sorín and Raúl de la Torre and on Bebe Kamín's *Los chicos de la guerra* (1984). María Esther Palant made *Riganelli* (1963) and *La conquista de la Pampa* (1967) before moving to Peru in 1966, where she taught film at the Universidad de Lima (Seibel 124). She has since made many shorts on artists, including *Cántico de color y luz* (1978), which she filmed in Argentina. *Riganelli* documents, in thirteen minutes, the life and work of the Argentine sculptor Agustín Riganelli (Centro de las Artes de Expresión Audiovisual 36), while the ten-minute *La conquista de la Pampa* is based on *La guerra al malón*, by Comandante Manuel Prado (Fondo Nacional de las Artes n.d., 20), a classic chronicle of the genocidal military campaigns of the late nineteenth century. *Cántico de color y luz*, also at ten minutes, features "the stained-glass windows painted by the Austrian Adolfo Winternitz. The fragments of his works, a few images of the artist in his workshop, classical music and the poetic voice accompany the development of the short that attempts to offer a vision on the work of a little-known artist" (Campo 45). Palant went on to further activities in the cinema, including work as a scenographer (Campo 44).

In further work produced by the FNA, Diana Ferraro, who had studied at the Escuela de Cine at the Universidad Nacional de La Plata (Truglio 318), made *Primera Exposición Representativa de Artesanías Argentinas* (1968), a ten-minute documentary on the eponymous exhibition that was organized by the FNA (Fondo Nacional de las Artes n.d., 39). She worked for several years in documentary and newsreel production, before beginning a long career in essay and fiction writing. Mara Horenstein made the sixteen-minute *Aída Carballo y su mundo* (1970), which documents the life and work of the Argentine visual artist who thematized the mental illness from which she suffered (Fondo de Cultura Nacional, *Cineteca* 13). In the film, "we see the artist in her 'world': the house, her workshop in San Telmo, everything we see re-created in her work. Throughout the film, texts by Aída Carballo are heard in the voice of María Rosa Gallo" (Ministerio de Cultura y Educación 19). The film responds formally to Carballo's work, as Campo comments: "A group of actors represents the attitudes of the insane gathered in an open patio, who are filmed with a wide-angle lens that produces a stretching of the images, mostly faces in close-up. The same effect is used by Carballo in her pictorial representations and engravings of characters" (Campo 48). María Esther Bianchi made the fourteen-minute *Las catorce estaciones* (1977), which documents, at the yearly Easter festival in Tilcara, a small town in the Quebrada de Humahuaca, "the making of large liturgical panels—chapels or shrines—constructed with natural flower petals, seeds, tree bark, etc., that the town honors in procession" (Fondo Nacional de las Artes n.d., 74). Marilyn Contardi, who had studied at the Escuela Documental de Santa Fe, directed, under the auspices of the FNA, the ten-minute *Al sur de Santa Fe* (1978), and has since directed many more documentaries. Concepción Prat Gay de Constenla made *Allpa Tupak/Tierra prodigiosa* and *Al corazón de las kenas* in the 1960s. These films, the first at seventeen minutes and the second at ten minutes, are documentaries "on the natural beauty of our northern provinces and some of their folkloric aspects" (Fondo Nacional de las Artes n.d., 35–36).[29] Finally, Lita Stantic codirected *El bombero está triste y llora* (1965) with Pablo Szir. Of the women who directed shorts under the auspices of the FNA, Stantic was the only one to go on to direct a feature.

While these makers of short films treated the format as a means to document, to denounce social inequalities, or eventually move to features, by the late 1960s several Argentine filmmakers began to employ the format as a medium for aesthetic experimentation. Among these were Marie-Louise Alemann and Narcisa Hirsch, who self-financed their experimental films made on Super 8 and 16-millimeter film.[30]

Experimental film resists definition, but contact between the following two passages from important practitioners of the form, one from Argentina and the other from the United States, can serve to explain the motivations, methods, and increased aesthetic possibilities that define it:

> Productions in Super 8 need not answer to any union of technicians. Nor of artists, distributors or exhibitors. Nor must they pass under the nose of any censor du jour. Nor pay taxes. Super 8 demands a different relation with the cinema, from its conception to its screening. It allows for unprecedented exhibition circuits. Which? Those that its makers imagine and make happen. It is they who choose the kind of film they make, its audiences and the way to reach them. A self-determination that many professionals would bless. Super 8 demands a rediscovery of the possibilities of the craft. The veterans of 35mm sigh: "Today anyone makes films . . ." That's exactly what it's about. (Caldini 31)

> If a film fails to take advantage of the self-existing magic of things, if it uses objects merely to mean something, it has thrown away one of its great possibilities. (Dorsky 38)

The juxtaposition of these passages is meant to elicit resonances between the thoughts of two experimental filmmakers, from different hemispheres, whose filmmaking practice shares many aspects. The first, Claudio Caldini, speaks of the autonomy offered by small-gauge film, which has allowed him and others to privilege what the second, Nathaniel Dorsky, calls the "self-existing magic of things." The idea that artistic possibility expands in an inverse relation to costs may seem obvious on reflection—and is cherished by makers and viewers of experimental film—but it is ignored by the vast majority of film viewers and irrelevant to those filmmakers who serve them.

As may be obvious, many of the increased possibilities brought about by low-cost filmmaking are political, but others are aesthetic. When one hears mention of a filmic avant-garde of the 1960s and 1970s in Latin America, the first models that come to mind are usually Solanas and Getino's "Third Cinema," Glauber Rocha's "Aesthetic of Hunger," or Julio García Espinosa's "Imperfect Cinema," each a theorization of a Latin American politically militant cinema. These models were part of a continent-wide search for a powerful filmic language that would forward the struggle for continental liberation, but the other Latin American avant-garde cinema—which might be more properly described as experimental—instead of taking up militancy, privileged vision over revolution and poetic resonance over shock montage.

The 1970s experimental film scene in Argentina is not widely known, but its existence in a culturally sophisticated metropolis like Buenos Aires should not be at all surprising. It flowered, faded, then disappeared from memory, but in recent years has seen a resurgence in visibility with screenings, several home video releases, and scholarly research. The scene was never well documented in its own time, a point Hirsch, who is one of its two most well-known filmmakers (the other is Caldini), makes by comparing it to New York's thriving experimental scene, which she knew well from having often spent time there: "I saw how [Jonas] Mekas's organization worked. . . . There were debates, books were written. Here nothing was ever written, no review was ever published. There Mekas published a weekly column in the *Village Voice* . . . it was something that lots of people read, thousands and thousands of people. Here no one ever published anything about us" (Paparella 68). While the contrast may appear exaggerated, it is undeniable that the Buenos Aires experimental filmmakers were relatively isolated. Even within the local film scene their public was very limited in comparison to that of more political filmmakers, their projects less about using film as a political tool than as a means to create novel, immediate experiences by privileging vision, poetic resonance, and exploration of the medium's specificity. While certainly not activists of the political left, even disavowing the connection between their work and politics, it could be said that they practiced a different ethics of the image from what Solanas and Getino called first (industrial), second (auteur), and third (militant) cinemas.[31]

The small community of filmmakers eventually became known as the Grupo Goethe, in a reference to the Instituto Goethe of Buenos Aires, which provided legitimization by association during the dictatorship and material support in the form of workshops and a screening space. Several members of the group had been on the margins of the much more publicly visible artistic underground centered on the Instituto Di Tella, but at moments of increased political violence and state repression—especially during the government of Isabel Perón (1974–1976) and the military dictatorship that followed—the underground would disperse (Denegri 97). The Grupo Goethe corresponds mostly to these phases, during which several of the filmmakers turned to more low-profile filmmaking that did not engage with national or continental political imperatives, but instead shared in the aesthetic priorities of a widely dispersed, but never numerous, international community of experimental filmmakers. The appeal of experimental film has, after all, always been limited to a very restricted public, and innovations within it pass slowly, if at all, beyond its restricted field to the wider cinematic culture.

Like most experimental film practice, Hirsch's work has rarely crossed beyond the confines of a very limited local scene, but it is arguably the most important body of work within that scene. Although it has circulated both within Argentina and internationally in the past several years, I will, without making larger claims for her work's impact, examine how Hirsch's filmmaking has inhabited the Argentine experimental scene and how its innovations result in a unique exploration of gendered subjectivity that privileges the body and the personal. Hirsch employs strategies of authorial self-inscription that include self-portraiture, autobiography, and the private-sphere domesticity often typical of work in smaller-gauge film. These strategies contest the conventions of an experimental scene in which women were seldom the subject of vision, and which tended to eschew the quotidian to instead explore the specificities of the medium itself, an aesthetic exemplified most notably in the Argentine context in work by Caldini and in Hirsch's own early work.

Scholarship on experimental film often takes up the terms used to describe the works of the filmmakers based in New York, with P. Adams Sitney's *Visionary Cinema* (first published in 1974) providing many of them. Since Argentine experimental filmmakers' exposure to films by Jonas Mekas, Michael Snow, Andy Warhol, and others—both in occasional public screenings and through Hirsch's private archive—deeply informed their own work, they share in the models, intentions, and techniques that were part of the fairly universal vocabulary of experimental film by the 1970s. Therefore, as long as care is taken to not reduce the specificity of these works made in such a different context, it would be counterproductive to renounce adjectives like "structural" and "diary" in referring to the films of the Grupo Goethe.

Hirsch began working in film in the late 1960s, after she, Alemann, and other artists arranged for several of their performance pieces, or "happenings," to be filmed, but she soon turned to what could more conventionally be called experimental film. Her early films function fully within the aesthetic of the structural film, a term coined by Sitney to refer to a cinema "in which the shape of the whole film is predetermined and simplified, and it is that shape which is the primal impression of the film. . . . The structural film insists on its shape, and what content it has is minimal and subsidiary to the outline" (348). Structural film is seen as guided by a modernist imperative of medium-specific purification, the "reduction of the art object to the essential physical or material components of its medium" (Walley 17). In the most well-known explorations of the material parameters of the medium—Snow's *Wavelength* (1967) and *La région centrale* (1971), Ernie Gehr's *Serene Velocity* (1970), and Hollis Frampton's *Zorn's Lemma* (1970) and *(nostalgia)* (1971)—improvisation is banished and formal structure is carefully, even mathematically planned. In order to produce their very uncommon cinematic experiences, instead of constructing coherent diegetic worlds (as in most narrative film) or, alternatively, surrealist spatial discontinuity (as in certain films of the historical avant-garde), structural films often create incoherent spaces that challenge the viewer's ability to self-orient, then employ duration to elicit emotional and psychological responses and call the viewer's attention to his or her own defamiliarized perceptual process.

Hirsch's *Come out* (1971) does just this. Its soundtrack is Steve Reich's piece of the same name, in which a short clip of sound—a voice saying "come out"—is repeated, with increasing distortion through time. Before long the phonemes become unrecognizable, melding into a kind of pure, unsignifying sound as the figurative becomes abstract and communication cedes to something more like hypnosis. Meanwhile, the image progresses in the opposite direction, from abstraction toward figuration. Of the two shots in the film, the first is a fixed-camera long take that begins so out of focus as to be abstract. Very gradual manipulations of lighting, focus, and telephoto lens (in a slow zoom out) eventually make the image readable, and from cognitive chaos emerges a low-level epiphany: a needle skipping on a long-play record becomes visible, a possible source of the sound. In a second shot, the camera is tilted vertically down at a spinning record that comes to a stop with the label reading "Steve Reich, Come Out." But this visual explanation is not definitive, since the process has introduced doubt. The film prompts its viewer to ask if the distortions to the sound are happening in the film or in the viewer's own head, which has by now been shown to be as much a part of the cinematic apparatus as the camera, the projector, and the phonograph.

Several years after *Come out*, Hirsch made *Taller* (1975), a film inspired, according to Hirsch, by a description of Snow's *A Casing Shelved* (1970), in which an image of a bookshelf is accompanied by the filmmaker's voiced description of the objects seen. In *Taller*, apart from a slight opening camera movement and some shifts in illumination, the image is static, a small section of a wall in Hirsch's studio, covered in photographs and other objects gathered by her, and which thus call forth, qua madeleine, memories from her own past. A disembodied woman's voice (it is that of the filmmaker herself) is heard describing what the viewer sees and offering backstories to the photos and objects.

As Kaja Silverman writes, referring to the disruption of a convention that holds for both narrative and experimental film, to allow a woman's voice to be heard without showing her image "would disrupt the specular regime upon which dominant cinema relies; it would put her beyond the reach of the male gaze . . . and release her voice from the signifying obligations which that gaze enforces. It would liberate the female subject from the interrogation about her place, her time, and her desires which constantly resecures her. Finally, to disembody the female voice in this way would be to challenge every conception by means of which we have previously known woman within Hollywood film, since it is precisely *as body* that she is constructed there" (164; emphasis in original). For Silverman, to disembody the female voice is to free it, and thus render it dangerous. Without a signifying body, it would present to a spectator a blank canvas on which to construct a subjectivity, thus an object to be grappled with on unfamiliar ground.

In *Taller*, Hirsch engages with this disembodiment in a deceptively complex way. Her own voice begins by accurately describing what is visible in the frame—an accuracy that authorizes this voice despite its gender—then goes on to describe the other, unseen walls of the studio, thus authoring the unseen image through a channel that is conventionally rendered superfluous, subordinated to the image. As such, *Taller* breaks with the iconography of the feminine as object, rather than as subject. Such a use of voice-over supplements the kind of medium-specific purification seen earlier in *Come out* and, by introducing improvisation, overflows the structuralist conventions, which are incapable of containing the female subjectivity expressed that flows from Hirsch's lived experience.

Along with *Come out*, *Taller* could be considered a transition from Hirsch's earlier, outward-looking underground films to the inward gaze of certain experimental films of the Grupo Goethe. Her earliest films, those that documented the late-1960s happenings, privileged an imperative to make oneself visible, to be out in the streets of the city, while the treatment of space in *Taller*, made in a political context in which calling attention to oneself in public was already unwise, is a turn inward in a double sense, both spatial and personal.[32] The first turn is toward the domestic space inhabited by the filmmaker—her studio—and the second a fragmentary exploration of her own interiority, that of a woman and an artist, a diaristic aspect that will run through much of her work to follow.

After these two works, both filmed on 16 millimeter, that engage with the principles of structural film, Hirsch makes an important artistic break with a shift to working on Super 8 film and an aesthetic turn away from medium-specific purification toward what could be called an impure medium specificity, in a productive response to the Super 8 medium's generative qualities. Made possible by the portability and ease of use of Super 8, the impurity is produced by the improvised filming of the objects of the reality of the filmmaker's life. But her response is not limited to the convenient filming of objects that, if economics and portability allowed, she could have filmed on 16 or 35 millimeter. Hirsch produces an aesthetic response to the particularities of Super 8 film that reveals affinities to her artistic beginnings as a painter, a point on which I differ from Bernini's opinion that in Hirsch's case "it is impossible to consider her shorts through any aesthetic originating in the visual arts, but, rather, they are part of the properly cinematographic tradition of experimental film" (2013, 11). While I agree with Bernini's assertion that Hirsch's aesthetic is highly influenced by existing experimental works such as Mekas's diary films, I would add that starting with *Testamento y vida interior* (1977), but especially in *Homecoming* (1978), there is in her images a presence of the materiality of the Super 8 medium and its properties as distinct from 16 or 35 millimeter, both of which are generally used in a more transparent way. Here Hirsch's attention to materiality does not manifest itself structurally, as it did in *Come out* and *Taller*, nor in the explicit ways in which, say, Stan Brakhage scratches directly onto the celluloid strip or Jean-Luc Godard deconstructs the building blocks of filmic illusionism one by one. It happens, rather, within the filmed images themselves.

In a filmic textural equivalent of conspicuous brush strokes, the grain and softness of small-gauge film combine with a deliberate and consistent use of light and shadow, shifts in focus, and single-frame exposure and other film-speed effects to produce a texture that at moments pushes the figurative toward abstraction. This aesthetic rejects transparency, but instead of merely calling attention to the material parameters of Super 8 film, it produces a beauty specific to it. Bernini's characterization of Hirsch's work as partaking in "experimental beauty"—"the beauty that experimental film can offer"—is felicitous. The texture that results from the palpability of the Super 8 material support mediates between the viewer and the people, places and objects seen, calling attention to the qualities of the medium (as structural film had done) as it produces a beauty specific to its images. Other than occasional exceptions that, if isolated from their context, might feel like Kodak moments—backlit blond hair blowing in the breeze—Hirsch's images are neither classical nor clichéd, but are strong, visceral images made even more so by her aesthetic. The few images that might feel clichéd go on to resonate against images that depict human cruelty on a scale both intimate and historic (which Bernini refers to as "sublime cruelty"), and which, being part of this counterpoint, are recoded in *Homecoming* and after as part of a tragic and complex whole.

Homecoming contains a diary film—defined by Sitney as "quotidian lyrics, spontaneous, perhaps tentative, records of a sensibility in the midst of, or fresh from, experience" (424)—in which the montage, which might appear to be based on chance, is inevitably guided by the quotidian experiences of the film's author. It consists of diaristic images shot in Patagonia: a slaughtered lamb, a baby being born and nursing. Liquids, flows, and cycles dominate images that at times edge toward illegibility. As the film builds up its collage of diverse kinds of imagery, some of the individuals seen reappear, others do not. The qualities of the images also vary widely, from sharp and transparent to out of focus, underlit, and on the edge of abstraction, and there are no indications or continuity editing that might locate the images in time and space. To borrow the words of Alison Butler, here the self-inscription does not imply "the construction of a coherent subject position for the author, but the construction of a viable speaking position which, nonetheless, mirrors and enacts the author's experience of selfhood and embodiment as multiple and fragmented" (61). Such a description of authorial performativity in experimental film is an apt characterization of Hirsch's densely textured diary films, composed of images that might mimic the workings of memory while refusing to postulate a stable identity and defusing the kind of truth claims associated with more militant filmmaking, work on national memory, or even certain more subjective documentaries.

Homecoming explores with great affective power certain dimensions that Argentine cinema would regularly explore by the new millennium: domesticity in a realist, nonidealized key, the intimate world of women, doubts about memories and about what is seen in the very images themselves, which are no longer transparent windows onto the real, due to texture, tight framing, errant focus, fragmenting montage, and the elliptical nature of the stories it almost tells. Hirsch has continued to make films, and in recent years her work has been screened and written about more frequently.[33]

The final filmmaker I will address in this chapter is the one who has had the most lasting impact on Argentine cinema, but this is due more to her work as a producer than as a director. After studying at the Asociación de Cine Experimental, Lita Stantic codirected shorts in the 1960s and participated in the clandestine groups that screened *La hora de los hornos* (Eseverri and Peña 95–96). She has since worked extensively as a producer and directed the feature *Un muro de silencio* in 1993. With Bemberg, she founded GEA Cinematográfica, which produced the first five of Bemberg's six features, and she has since been the enabling force behind many ambitious films, among them some of the most significant works by women, including those by Lucrecia Martel, Lucía Cedrón, and Paz Encina. Stantic applies productive criteria to her selection of projects, which Constanza Burucúa describes as "the kind of cinema that she believes in and that she repeatedly refers to as 'necessary': a cinema of untold stories, of alternative points of view, of defiant approaches to a continually changing reality" (215). Such criteria have resulted in the production of many films that might have otherwise gone unmade, since through her unique production work Stantic added space to a limited field of filmmaking, space in which were made several of the most important films of what would become known as the Nuevo Cine Argentino (Burucúa 223).

A possible impulse behind Stantic's efforts to help women direct is mentioned in the autobiographical section of the book *Lita Stantic: El cine es automóvil y poema*. She describes the early obstacles she faced as created by a pervasive institutional patriarchy within the cinema industry, exemplified by the advice given to her by a producer the first time she asked to attend a day of filming: "You're wasting your time: the cinema isn't for women" (qtd. in Eseverri and Peña 83). Thanks to Stantic's stubborn efforts and expansive criteria, many filmmakers have been able to work in the last forty years, including several of today's most important women directors, but she is also a filmmaker in her own right.

Before directing *Un muro de silencio*, one of the key films on memory made in the decades following the dictatorship, she codirected, with Pablo Szir, several shorts in the mid-1960s. The first was *El bombero está triste y llora* (1965), made on 35-millimeter film and funded by the Fondo Nacional de las Artes. As Stantic describes the short, "The idea was to work with the way kids discover light, darkness and colors from the elements that surround them" (qtd. in Eseverri and Peña 91). Through expressive camerawork and music, the film represents children's perceptions and imagination as a defamiliarizing mediator between reality and artistic production. *Un día* (1966), made on 16-millimeter film, recreates a day in the life of a kindergarten child. Discussing the editing of *Un día*, Stantic tells of another example of a male film professional closing a door to a woman: "Antonio Ripoll did the editing. . . . I remember I told him I wanted to learn editing by working with him. At first he agreed, but then he called me to say that his partner, Gerardo Rinaldi, didn't want him to. He didn't want women on the team" (91). Sexism in film production is here seen to extend beyond the industry to the more independent sector (Ripoll was an early participant at the Escuela Documental de Santa Fe), where it has since been partly overcome, in large part due to the efforts of Stantic herself as producer. Burucúa summarizes

Stantic's attitude toward gender: "Whenever she decides to produce a film directed by a woman, the decision to embark on such projects does not necessarily stem from the fact that the script is written by a woman but, mostly, from her impression that they advance a novel, and generally defiant, take on a particular issue, that they will become what she identifies as 'necessary' films. It is precisely this understanding of a film being socially necessary that summarizes her ethical commitment to both cinema and reality" (222). This imperative to produce necessary films that generate new perspectives is also evidenced in the founding in 1988 of the Asociación La Mujer y el Cine (Association "Woman and the Cinema") by Stantic, Bemberg, Marta Bianchi, and others. The association's festival organization, short film competitions, and prizes have played an important role in the recent success women have had in direction (Bettendorf and Pérez Rial 28–30; Rangil 162). Yet of the many films Stantic has produced, the most important impact, both in commercial terms and in that of the problematization of gender representation, remain those directed by Bemberg in the 1980s.

With this chapter I have tried to account as comprehensively as possible for the opportunities taken up by women in short filmmaking, often as a start of a career in cinema. During the 1960s there were doubtlessly other women who directed short films, and Vlasta Lah directed two features in the early 1960s. But it was only in the 1970s that women made more lasting inroads into feature film direction, with Landeck's *Gente en Buenos Aires* (1973) and María Herminia Avellaneda's *Juguemos en el mundo* (1971), which are discussed in chapters 2 and 3, respectively, before the period of relative opportunity for filmmakers that had lasted since the late 1950s came to an end with the censorship, blacklisting, and paramilitary and state terrorism of the Isabel Perón presidency and the subsequent military dictatorship.[34]

2
Eva Landeck

The cultural climate of the period beginning in 1966 with the Onganía dictatorship and running through the 1973 return of Perón to power, the 1976 coup, and the subsequent military dictatorship was, with brief exceptions, treacherous for cultural producers who strove to critically reflect Argentine reality. This was particularly true of those who worked in feature-length narrative film, long recognized by the state for its unique power to reach a wide audience. In her three feature films, Eva Landeck responded to the political conjuncture of the 1970s by exploring the condition of life under an authoritarian state, violence and all. She did so despite efforts, eventually successful, by that same power to thwart her creative freedom. In order to place Landeck and her films in their cultural field, a brief account of the political situation will be useful.

After the overthrow of Arturo Illia in 1966, Onganía sought to legitimize his power with plans to *frenar el desorden* (control disorder). The state waged a campaign against modern youth culture, going so far as to order the police to arrest young men with long hair and women who wore miniskirts, and took control of public universities, employing violence to do so in notorious episodes like the "Noche de los Bastones Largos" (Night of the batons) in July 1966. But opposition to the regime became increasingly widespread, especially after the Cordobazo uprising in May 1969 that, albeit temporarily, united working-class and student sectors.

Historians recognize several factors that contributed to this mobilization, but one of the most important was the confluence of formerly incompatible left sectors and Peronism as the general himself fanned the flames from exile in Madrid. In the early 1970s, "youth appears to become the privileged recipient of the leader's favors: He frequently celebrates the presence of youth at all the demonstrations of the Peronist movement and expresses support for the violent actions carried out by the youth groups" (Sigal and Verón 133).[1] With the kidnapping and killing of the former military dictator and fervent anti-Peronist Pedro Eugenio Aramburu by the revolutionary Peronist guerrilla Montoneros in May and June 1970—actions for which Perón expressed his approval—the climate of political violence took on a new intensity. Due to the history of repressive violence by the military, many Argentines saw Aramburu's killing as an act of popular justice. Marcos Novaro writes that according to surveys at the time, close to 50 percent of the population sympathized with the guerrillas (106). Especially for the young, opposition to the long-running alliance between traditional economic elites and the military became a generational imperative, and many participated in less violent direct actions, such as work in the *villas miseria* to both alleviate poverty and raise the political consciousness of their inhabitants.

As the long dictatorship led by Onganía, then Roberto Marcelo Levingston, then Alejandro Agustín Lanusse, dragged on, the country appeared less and less governable as the political opposition, increasingly in the form of the Juventud Peronista, coalesced around Perón and asserted itself. As Maristella Svampa writes, "Toward the end of 1972 the encounter between a mobilized society and the exiled leader took a new turn, marked by the Peronization of the heterogeneous field of the left. This confluence brought together different branches of syndicalism, vast sectors of the intellectual and artistic world—many of which had held strong anti-Peronist convictions until shortly before—wide portions of youth, social-Christian sectors, such as the Movement of Priests for the Third World, and much of the new urban guerrilla" (2003, 388–389). With such sympathies for the Peronist movement surging, even those in power came to recognize in its political participation the best chance to avoid social upheaval. As Perón's return began to appear inevitable, his encouragement for both left and right militants fueled incompatibilities internal to the movement that eventually led to a violent struggle between the more youthful Tendencia Revolucionaria and the orthodox right. As the Tendencia generated intense enthusiasm among many young Argentines, spreading its message of revolution through, among other avenues, the Montonero weekly *El Descamisado*, first published on May 8, 1973, the Peronist right responded with organizations and publications designed to directly counter them. The Juventud Peronista de la República Argentina was founded in 1973, and the rabid weekly *El Caudillo de la Tercera Posición* was first published on November 16, 1973, both funded by the Ministry of Social Welfare under José López Rega "to challenge the Revolutionary Tendency's representation of youth to Perón" (Marongiu 9). Around this time the *sinarquía* (synarchy) conspiracy theory became conspicuous in the right's discourse as a way to group its various perceived enemies under a single supranational entity that included Communists, Jews, Masons, and Liberals (Besoky 147).

In 1973 Peronism had been legalized, but Perón himself was not allowed to run for the presidency. His stand-in, Héctor Cámpora, won the election with the support of the Tendencia Revolucionaria and took office on May 25. The popular Peronist filmmakers Hugo del Carril and Mario Soffici were appointed to run the Instituto Nacional de Cinematografía, the state entity charged with regulating cinema production. Both production and attendance increased, and politically engaged films were made, many of which were commercially successful. In narrative film there was an opening for themes that until then had been untouchable, such as the historic rural labor conflicts fictionalized in *La Patagonia rebelde* (Héctor Olivera, 1974) and *Quebracho* (Ricardo Wullicher, 1974), as well as references to political violence, such as in Raymundo Gleyzer's *Los traidores* (1973) and Landeck's *Gente en Buenos Aires* (1973).

The *primavera camporista* ended abruptly. During Cámpora's brief administration the struggle internal to Peronism intensified, and when on June 20, 1973, Perón returned to Argentina, in the massive welcome at Ezeiza Airport the right-wing sectors attacked the crowds of supporters of the Tendencia Revolucionaria, killing more than a dozen and injuring hundreds. Perón himself soon broke with the Tendencia, forcing the resignation of Cámpora and calling for *depuración*, a purge, to eliminate communist "subversion" of the movement (Franco 202). In the ensuing election Perón ran for the presidency and won easily, with his wife, María Estela Martínez de Perón, or Isabel, as vice president. When, after serving less than ten months, he died on July 1, 1974, his widow took over the presidency. Under the sway of her adviser, José López Rega, a paramilitary apparatus, the Alianza Anticomunista Argentina (or Triple A), was set up to hunt down and eliminate opposition figures, and thus intimidate others who might consider participation in political militancy. In August 1974, Isabel Perón put the notorious extreme-right journalist Miguel Paulino Tato in charge of film censorship, which returned with a force greater than ever before. As Isabel's weakened government lost control of security and the economy, the armed forces took control on March 24, 1976, and set out to violently eliminate any resistance, which included all things not "Occidental and Christian," as the leader of the military junta, General Jorge Videla, declared. The armed forces implemented a *plan antisubversivo* that included kidnapping, torturing, and murdering not only the armed opposition but also, most notably, many union activists, students, professors, and cultural producers. In such a climate, involvement with any kind of militancy, even from not necessarily left positions such as feminism, was potentially dangerous. Films continued to be made, even some that set out to denounce the repression despite the state's vigilance regarding film production, but the dictatorship definitively shut down the cultural effervescence of the preceding decades.

During the 1960s and early 1970s, filmmaking in Argentina (as elsewhere) had undergone deep shifts that resulted in far greater possibilities than before and after, and much of what was made during the period came to be known as the Nuevo Cine (New Cinema, or on a continental scale, the Nuevo Cine Latinoamericano. Due to its politicization during such a conflictive period, scholars have been, understandably, quick to take up this cinema, generating a wealth of studies. With the recent expansion of scholarly attention to other periods and approaches, some revision of these earlier studies has taken place, to which this chapter intends to contribute by discussing the presence of a filmmaker who has not often been recognized, in large part due to the suppression and subsequent unavailability of her films and a not unrelated long-running critical neglect. Eva Landeck, as the third woman to direct a feature-length sound film in Argentina, set precedents for women in creative roles in the cinema at the same time that her films engaged profoundly with the politics of their time and the abuses of an increasingly authoritarian and violent state, yet she and her films are very seldom, if at all, mentioned in studies of the period.

The question of gender in the Nuevo Cine has largely been ignored by scholars, and Landeck goes undiscussed in most histories of political filmmaking, such as Lusnich and Piedras's two-volume *Una historia del cine político y social en Argentina* (2009, 2011), or in more general histories (Peña 2012). Zuzana Pick points out that the New Cinema films made by Latin American women are "characterized by an heterogeneity of modes of production and reception according to diverse national, institutional, and personal contexts and ideological objectives" (67). Although Pick is not referring specifically to Landeck, the production and reception of her films are uniquely revealing of the dynamics around gender, culture, and politics in the 1970s. Film production and screening in the context of political upheaval and military dictatorships is a courageous public act that in itself can be considered a statement on the possibility and legitimacy of women as artists, cultural producers, and active participants in the political realm.

After studying in the 1940s at the Facultad de Filosofía y Letras of the University of Buenos Aires, Landeck studied psychology at the Instituto Sigmund Freud. Then, as she tells it "I married very young, had children, worked to survive, and abandoned for a time my artistic restlessness" ("Eva Landeck: Gente en Buenos Aires" 20). She eventually studied filmmaking at the Asociación de Cine Experimental, also in Buenos Aires, from 1957 to 1962, after which she began to make short films (Trelles Plazaola 199). Her description of her training in filmmaking represents it as a fragmentary process, yet the only one available to her. She explains that after four years at the Asociación de Cine Experimental,

> I continued taking seminars and realized I knew very little. These were, of course, impoverished, minor schools with little material and very few professors. . . . . I was already thinking about the cinema, of course, and since there was no training in acting direction for film, I studied acting direction for theater, to later apply it to the cinema. . . . I still felt I was lacking other technical elements. Pablo Tabernero, . . . a great director of photography of the old Argentine cinema, worked in Alex Laboratories because he had gone blind. He started to offer classes at the industry union. . . . I was the only woman in the class, which I took despite the fact that I wasn't in the union. (Trelles Plazaola 197–199)

Landeck managed to piece together an education in feature filmmaking despite her gender, which condemned her to outsider status. This fragmentary, somewhat improvised training prefigures the situations in which she would work on her three features, none of which she made under an established producer.

In 1963 she made, for German television, a short documentary titled *Barrios y teatros de Buenos Aires*. By the mid-1960s she had moved on to the short fiction format, first with *Entremés* (1966), then *Horas extras* (1967) and *El empleo* (1970), before turning to feature-length filmmaking. Her first feature, *Gente en Buenos Aires*, was made in part during the cultural flourishing of the *primavera camporista*. She wrote the script in 1972 and, unable to find financial backing, devised a cooperative funding plan. Since the film industry was in a period of reduced production, several technicians and actors enthusiastically agreed to her plan, the implementation of which she describes as follows:

> No one was filming anything at that moment, and I had a little money. I went to the union, spoke with (the cinematographer Juan Carlos) Desanzo and (the actor Luis) Brandoni. . . . They were both very willing to work in a cooperative. Everything went very well. . . . They announced the project on the chalkboard of the union, to see who wanted to work in a cooperative. The response was very good. The lower-earning positions were paid, but the technicians had to join a kind of partnership. They were paid part of their salary weekly, and the rest went back into the cooperative. (Trelles Plazaola 200–201)

This self-generated production model gave Landeck extraordinary creative control over the project, and filming was completed in 1973 in the relatively open climate of the *primavera camporista*. But after completion the premiere was delayed several months when films made by larger producers (she specifically names Sergio Renán's *La tregua*) were given screening privilege over hers (Hardouin and Ivachow 49). By the time *Gente en Buenos Aires* opened in August 1974, Isabel Perón was president and censorship had taken on the direct form of intimidation and threats.[2] But the film opened well, according to Landeck, continuing to draw spectators and staying on screens for six weeks, before finally being pulled due to threats against its lead actor, Luis Brandoni, by the Triple A.[3] Landeck recounts that "they took it down right when they threatened Brandoni and he had to leave the country, a bad moment—1974—a date I'll never forget" (Trelles Plazaola 200–202).[4] As a result of these pressures, *Gente en Buenos Aires* vanished from view and remained little seen until recently.[5]

The social conflict, political militancy, and state violence of the early 1970s in Argentina are represented in several ways in *Gente en Buenos Aires*. The film intercuts two different registers: black-and-white newsreel footage is set against the narration, mostly in color, of a romance between Pablo (Brandoni) and Inés (Landeck's daughter Irene Morack), two young, middle-class internal migrants to the capital who work in precarious and unrewarding jobs in sales. The city is an alienating space that renders unlikely the kind of romance that drives most narrative films, including this one, due to the quotidian stresses and competition that drive intensely antagonistic interpersonal relations. Manners are brusque, interactions aggressive, and humiliation of the other is normalized in daily social intercourse. Inés, prompted by her colleagues at work, sharpens her incivility into a cutting cruelty toward the socially awkward Pablo during his commercial visits. But when he finds a certain Inés's phone number on a drawing she had made for the wife of his friend, Pablo calls her. Through long nightly conversations they bond and eventually fall in love, while failing to realize that they have already met. By chance, Pablo finds out who she is, and arranges a meeting. In an emotional final sequence in which, upon seeing Pablo, Inés becomes ashamed and runs away, they end up coming together. As they walk hand in hand along the sidewalk, this final color shot is intercut with black-and-white documentary footage of street protests and police repression, a rhetorical strategy to which I will return.

The narration is set entirely within the city, but despite its urban setting, the economic subjection of the inhabitants of the nation's marginal spaces—rural and *villa*—to the national elite is a central concern of the film. This pervasive injustice and the conflict it generates are represented in several ways. First, their effects are shown to extend to Pablo's interiority, as he is portrayed in two dream sequences as participating, albeit unconsciously, in militant operations, carrying out direct actions as an urban *guerrillero*. In the film's opening shot, unmarked as a dream until its end, with a machine gun he executes a lineup of bourgeois men and women; in a later dream he appears as a samurai and robs a bank to redistribute wealth to the urban poor of a *villa miseria*. These dreams portray guerrilla violence as socially just, suggesting that Pablo's unconscious desires have been mediated by news of the activities of armed militant groups like Montoneros, Fuerzas Armadas

Revolucionarias and the Ejército Revolucionario del Pueblo, but that these desires to actively participate have been repressed by the alienating reality of his dystopic urban surroundings.

The social conflict also appears through the use of documentary evidence. The setting of the film in 1972 is made explicit by the headline of a newspaper read by Pablo that states "Fugaron Guerrilleros del Penal de Rawson" (Guerrillas escaped from Rawson Penitentiary), a reference to the Massacre of Trelew in which, on August 22, 1972, nineteen escaped prisoners—militants in Montoneros, FAR, and ERP—were recaptured and extrajudicially executed on a military base in the south of the country. The headline adds immediacy to the intercut black-and-white newsreel footage that frequently interrupts the color footage of the fictional narrative. These montage sequences show urban scenes, football matches, and a newspaper headline reading, "Más Detenidos por Actividades Extremistas" (More detained for extremist activities), but mostly protests and police repression. Thus, they situate the narrative in the conflictive political reality of its time as well as producing montage effects that imbue the film with a political charge unique to its historical moment through the juxtaposition of the political struggle with activities, such as spectator sports, which are often thought to distract the population from its immediate reality. In addition, by bringing into contact spaces that are usually separate, the montage sequences suggest causal relations that implicate national elites in the perpetuation of economic injustice and structural violence. Such montage effects produced in a narrative film set in the present work in direct opposition to the conventional escapism of narrative cinema.

The use of archival news footage of popular uprisings and their violent repression at the hands of the state was seen in many militant films of the period, both narrative and nonnarrative, most famously in *La hora de los hornos* (1968), but also in *Ya es tiempo de violencia* (Enrique Juárez, 1969), *Argentina, mayo de 1969: El camino a la liberación* (Realizadores de Mayo, 1969), *Los traidores* (Raymundo Gleyzer, 1973), and others. The ideological charge of the inclusion of such footage in *Gente en Buenos Aires* is unequivocal.

The popular uprising known as the Cordobazo had taken place only five years before the making of the film, and similar episodes had followed in the years since. The historian Marcos Novaro summarizes the effect of the Cordobazo on the hopes of the revolutionary left: "It was a demonstration of strength for the revolutionaries, since for the first time, and spontaneously, they managed to include wide sectors of society in their ranks. From that moment on they gained confidence, interpreting events to mean that the country had entered a 'pre-revolutionary situation,' and they proclaimed that the next step would be to bring 'class war' on a national scale" (102). The temporary alliance between left militants and the working class produced much optimism, and the media, especially television, spread the images nationwide, as Jessica Stites Mor explains:

> It is clear that the journalists, photographers, and news media that documented the Cordobazo and participated in its unfolding meant to invoke the social memory of heroics from a past moment of solidarity and glory among the laboring classes. The journalist Roberto di Chiara's televised images of the assault on the city center and the subsequent military repression were a significant point of inflection in this struggle, unique in Argentina's history because of the way that the conflict was captured by and broadcast over the national media, almost in real time. His footage captured a specific narrative of the conflict that celebrated the worker and emphasized the repressive nature of the state's intervention, a triumphalist vision that suggested an opportunity for radical action to make real change. (2012, 27)

The rapid, wide diffusion of Di Chiara's footage—including a charge by mounted police that suddenly shifts into a retreat in the face of the protesters, taking on a powerful allegorical charge—"exposed the weaknesses and excesses of Onganía's dictatorship" (27) as it recalled the public exercise of popular power so important to the first Peronist period, thus spurring optimism and further mobilization against state repression.

Landeck's use of newsreel footage of the Cordobazo and other episodes of repression and protest is, then, a highly politicized choice, one that locates *Gente en Buenos Aires* within this climate of optimism on the left and in sympathy with openly militant films that employed the same footage: "Mass media images of the Cordobazo . . . circulated a utopian political vision of popular rebellion that was easily recycled as stock footage for documentary and political filmmakers who had previously had to rely more heavily on propagandist newsreels for historical images. The television and print media manufactured an expansive collection of audiovisual material that filmmakers could use to reflect on and then represent the lived experiences of the period. This synergetic relationship would feed a hungry audience of leftist intellectuals, university students, labor activists, and their allies" (Stites Mor 2012, 28). While such borrowing of this footage was common among militant filmmakers of the time, the use of it by Landeck, as a less explicitly militant, narrative filmmaker, was a uniquely loaded choice.[6] In *Gente en Buenos Aires*, the black-and-white imagery is of a different order than the color sequences of the narration it interrupts, and as such is clearly marked as documentary registration of the kind of political militancy that Argentine fiction film had until recently avoided. The newsreel footage contextualizes the story of urban alienation and romance in a tense climate of political violence unique to its moment. This inclusion of footage proper to what is known as "third," or anticolonial, cinema makes *Gente en Buenos Aires* unique as a film that was screened in commercial theaters that more typically showed industrial or auteurist cinema.

The relationship to militant cinema is further consolidated by a profound exploration of the possibility, brought to the fore by the Cordobazo and advocated in militant cinema, of cross-class solidarity and the revolutionary potential of the popular classes. *Gente en Buenos Aires* elaborates on these shared interests by portraying both middle and working classes as victims of the entrenched economic power that led the country through a flawed modernization, periodic military governments, and the continued imposition of an alienating political and economic order. For the young protagonists, then, the class struggle can present a possible source of salvation from this order.

While the filmmakers of the Generación del 60 had exhaustively explored the theme of urban alienation, *Gente en Buenos Aires* widens its perspective to include the exploitative relationship between rural and urban spaces and the resulting political violence. Rural space is present, though always off-screen, and despite its dystopian portrait of the city, the film does not indulge in the facile antimodern nostalgia for rural space of the *criollista* imagery that characterized much of Argentine culture, and especially cinema, throughout the twentieth century. On several occasions it is suggested that the off-screen rural space is a site of human suffering due to exploitation by economic power. In one instance, a letter to Inés from her mother reveals that her family had owned a plot of land in the provinces, but they were forced to sell it during a drought, after which they were hired by the new owner to cultivate the same land. The transformation of Inés's family from landholders to laborers employed by capital suggests that this is an instance of speculative investment, the kind of dispossession that will not lead to greater economic justice or prosperity and as such cannot be considered a legitimate form of national modernization.

The critique of economic exploitation and the resulting conflict and political violence are made explicit in the discourse of Pablo's neighbor, Torres, a migrant from the rural interior whose status as popular advocate for social justice and possible political militant authorizes his discourse. While the usual authorized perspective is urban, that of either an intellectual or a member of the working class, Landeck's use of Torres provides a rural-based perspective less often seen in Argentine cinema. Through Torres's brief, colorful, and lucid account of class relations in Argentine society, rural space becomes the source of a more authentic social consciousness otherwise inaccessible to the more alienated urban protagonists. He lays out a simple but cogent account of the economic injustice brought about by Argentina's faulty modernization and an implicit justification of political militancy in a response to Pablo's complaint about the lack of free time suffered by city dwellers, saying that

> en el campo sobra el tiempo, y eso tampoco está bien. Al campo y a la ciudad hay que transformarlos para que la gente que trabaja tenga una vida humana. El hombre necesita tanto la naturaleza como la compañía de la gente. Y a nosotros nos toca vivir en un mundo de veinticinco millones de habitantes, y más de cincuenta millones de vacas.

> out in the country there's too much time, and that's not good either. The country and the city need to be transformed so that working people can have a humane life. Man needs nature as much as he needs the company of others. And we live in a world of twenty-five million inhabitants and more than fifty million cows.

The Torres character recalls the resistant *gaucho malo* of the nineteenth-century literary tradition, in which rural poverty and state violence are brought about by the national modernization project. Through Pablo's conversations with Torres, he is shown to undergo a process of conscientization regarding economic injustice that will soon take on a far darker tone. To Pablo's subsequent complaint, "yo no tengo ninguna vaca" (but I don't have any cows), Torres responds by quoting a song, written and made famous by Atahualpa Yupanqui, that denounces economic injustice: "Y yo tampoco, las vaquitas son ajenas" (Me neither, the cows belong to others).[7] Meanwhile, the filmmaker illustrates Torres's discourse by intercutting the shots of the conversation with documentary footage of livestock at the Sociedad Rural, thus identifying the exploitative economic power with the association of traditional wealthy landowners. Newsreel footage of protests and state violence is also shown, which anchors Torres's discourse in the national reality of the post-Cordobazo present and resonates unavoidably with *La hora de los hornos*, in which the landowning class of the Sociedad Rural is blamed for Argentina's uneven modernization and ridiculed as Eurocentric and superficial.

The most disturbingly prescient implications of the film are not reached until Pablo witnesses the violent abduction of Torres by what appears to be a paramilitary group. Pablo calls Torres's lawyer, whom he had met briefly, but is snubbed, prompting the viewer to the conclusion that the lawyer either informs for the abductors or is too fearful to pursue the case. Even as the romantic story line is resolved, Torres's fate is left unknown, like that of many of those who would be abducted and disappeared in the ensuing years. By the time of the film's release, during the presidency of Isabel Perón, the abduction and torture of citizens was already an established practice, although not yet at the levels it would soon reach. Most notoriously, it was carried out by the paramilitaries of the Triple A, organized by José López Rega, the minister of social welfare. Yet despite the increasing presence of such violence, it had seldom been referred to in narrative films set in the present.[8]

In certain aspects, *Gente en Buenos Aires* is in continuity with many of the narrative films of the auteur (or "second") cinema of the preceding fifteen years, but its representation of the intersection of space, economics, and political violence goes further. Many of the urban-set films of the Generación del 60 told stories of alienated yet comfortably middle-class youthful protagonists, though they frequently included passing references to the nation's economic inequalities. In *Los jóvenes viejos* (Rodolfo Kuhn, 1961), for example, the protagonists drive through a *villa miseria*, which is filmed from their passing car. In a similar strategy, the protagonists of *Prisioneros de una noche* (David José Kohon, 1962) travel by train through a *villa* that is conspicuously visible through the windows. As in many of the early features of the urban directors of the Generación del 60, the representation of the spatial margins does not extend much beyond this kind of background documentation.[9] Landeck's film, made at a more politically exacerbated moment, delves into the causes of the nation's uneven modernization and directly addresses the use of state violence to perpetuate social inequalities. But in addition to these themes, not uncommon in films around the time of the *primavera camporista*, Landeck extends the critique beyond the conflict between capital and labor, into the dynamic of dispossession that has since become central, as addressed by David Harvey in his account of "accumulation by dispossession." As Maristella Svampa wrote in 2015, the dynamic of dispossession has gone unaddressed even on the left: "A large part of the Latin American Left and progressive populism has maintained a productivist vision of development, which tends to privilege the conflict between capital and labor, minimizing or giving little attention to new social struggles concentrated on territory and the commons. In this political-ideological framework dominated by the productivist vision, the current dynamic of dispossession becomes a nonconceptualizable blind spot" (70). This blind spot was already addressed by Landeck with the episode of the dispossession of Inés's family's land, a point of intersection of the larger dynamics of capital accumulation, resistance, and state violence, at a moment in which these themes were uniquely immediate, shortly before the state neutralized the political struggle and rendered social issues unrepresentable. An examination of the following years of her career makes it clear that, as a result of its prescience in denouncing state violence, Landeck's *opera prima* was the beginning of the end of a very promising filmmaking career.

Between the making of *Gente en Buenos Aires* and Landeck's final films, the political situation underwent a drastic turn for the worse, with the presidency of Juan D. Perón and that of his widow, Isabel, under whom far-right sectors gained control over an increasingly repressive state, and the military coup of March 24, 1976. Fernando Varea emphasizes the differences between the periods before and after the 1976 coup: "It could be said that during the constitutional government of 1973–1976—with the coming together of the politicized atmosphere with freedom of expression and the generalized opinion that the pueblo and social needs should be a central consideration of artistic expressions—many concerns emerged, with undoubtable signs of renovation and commitment, for example, in education, journalism, theater, literature or popular music" (15). This was the period in which *Gente en Buenos Aires* was made and screened, and the social concerns mentioned by Varea are explicit on the surface in that film. In the post-coup period that followed, however, this kind of treatment became impossible: "The military dictatorship set out to erase all that with one stroke. The methods it used: expulsions, arrests, forced closures, prohibitions, kidnappings, death and disappearance of persons. In a short time, a valuable generation of artists and intellectuals disappeared from the media, although it was not only those absences that revealed the change: there was also a climate of militarization and subjugation" (15). Unlike under Onganía, this dictatorship's resolute campaign to eliminate all resistance rendered direct political messaging impossible. The subjugation referred to by Varea is personified in the realm of cinema by the notorious Miguel Paulino Tato, who had been appointed director of the Ente de Calificación Cinematográfica (Cinema Ratings Entity) under Isabel Perón and remained in the post until 1978. Tato's vision of the duty of a censor is made clear in a declaration he pronounced shortly before the coup of 1976: "I'm right in the middle of the action . . . and as long as they don't throw me out I'll keep carrying out this patriotic duty. I'm a free public servant and I'm carrying out prevention and hygiene in the cinema. I also have the support of the Army, the curia and above all the Argentine pueblo and families" (qtd. in Gociol and Invernizzi 37). This list of backers of Tato's prophylactic efforts points to certain sacred cows toward which questioning fingers could not be pointed in the cinema of the time: the military's legitimization as a necessary force of order, the church's role as unblemished moral compass, the glorious image of the pueblo, and the centrality of the normative family to the integrity of the national society.

After *Gente en Buenos Aires*, Landeck made two films under dictatorship, one in Argentina and the other in Uruguay. After she drew the Argentine censor's attention to herself with her first film, the state compromised her creative control, and Landeck herself considers both films flawed (Trelles Plazaola), as does Varea, who describes the plot of *Ese loco amor loco*, first screened on September 27, 1979: "One of the points of the far-fetched plot . . . was the search for the protagonist's sister, because of which suspicious or dangerous people were mentioned, with brief references to prostitution and drugs without ever using these two words themselves" (36). Varea's description perceptively notes the disappeared character, suspicions, and oblique references, but, not engaging with these more deeply, he dismisses the plot as nonsensical.

I would argue that the absences and oblique references of Landeck's last two films are products of a strategic authorship, operating within the limits imposed by the censors, that sets out to explore the mediation of the relationship between the military dictatorship and society by what Pilar Calveiro calls the *poder desaparecedor*, the power "to make disappear that which is dysfunctional, which in the [concentration] camp is the cadaver and in society the opposition, through a generalized terror that paralyzes, immobilizes, stuns" (1998, 156). This terror, addressed to society at large, sends a message that makes the dictatorship's "disciplinary and murdering power" (154) an open secret, as a "known-yet-denied reality" (147). This reality is known by all, yet it remains unmentioned due to the paralyzing fear it evokes, with the end result of eliminating all references to itself.

Calveiro describes how the disciplinary effects of the concentration camp are designed to flow outward into society as a whole and there produce silence. The concentration camp "can only exist in a society that chooses not to see, due to its own powerlessness ... as stunned as the captives themselves" (1998, 147). In Argentina, the fact of the clandestine detention centers, then, generated a society-wide fear that rendered unrepresentable the military's widely known illicit practices. Stunned into speechlessness, "the society as a whole accepted the incongruency between the discourse and the political practice of the military, between public and private life, between what is said and what is ignored as a form of self-preservation" (151). This incongruence between discourse and practice created a crisis of representation by discursively eliminating the actions of the state under the dictatorship, but despite such a climate, certain filmmakers managed to translate a critical impulse into film.

The effects on representation of the *poder desaparecedor* are built into the plot of *Ese loco amor loco* in the form of conspicuous silences and misdirection. On several occasions the film represents events similar to the real results of repressive actions of the military, only to have transparently unreliable characters attribute them to transparently false causes. Thus is formulated a central enigma, to which the obvious solution that goes unsaid is the "known-yet-denied reality" of the violence of the armed forces that was at its apogee as the film was made in the initial years of the dictatorship.

The implied contract of knowing-yet-denial under which the characters operate is laid bare for the viewer, who, in order to make sense of what happens yet is left unsaid, must acknowledge the pressure of the *poder desaparecedor* that makes state violence unspeakable. The film reflects, then, the dictatorship's strategy of self-representation, as described by Claudio Uriarte: "By day the Military Junta was the Dr. Jekyll of the moderation and professionalism of General Videla, only to turn into the multiform sinister storm of the task forces at night. The official country became the diurnal country and the real country was the nocturnal one, although fundamentally these two elements complemented and fed off one another" (166). The nocturnal dictatorship is the invisible mover that *Ese loco amor loco* can represent only by way of the effects of its actions.

The film tells the story of yet another protagonist who moves to the capital and undergoes a process of awakening. Emilia (Morack), a virginal and naive young woman from a small town, focalizes a narration of very limited omniscience, mostly restricted to her perspective, and the viewer is often given access to her mental subjectivity in the form of fantasies and daydreams fueled by literary classics like *Don Quijote* and *Anna Karenina*.

The plot of *Ese loco amor loco* is elliptical, and the motivation for story events often goes unaddressed or stated by characters who are rendered unreliable by what appears to be a fear of the *poder desaparecedor*. The disappearance of Lidia, the never-seen sister of Emilia, is the central example. At the beginning of the film her whereabouts are unknown, but her father has tried to convince

Emilia that Lidia's ex-husband, Andrés (played by Héctor Gióvine), is selling drugs, involved in pimping, and somehow to blame for her disappearance. Emilia's imagination runs wild at first, but she later finds these impressions and fears to be unfounded, and Andrés is instead shown to be an idealistic, even Quixotesque, scientist intent on developing a green technology to break down the discarded plastic bottles that abound in the diegesis. This is not the only story element that goes unexplained or unmotivated but which, if the extratextual reality of the time is considered, could readily be attributed to repressive actions of the state.

Since disappearances, extrajudicial killings, and university purges could not be represented on film, Landeck does not show, for example, Lidia being kidnapped. Instead, her disappearance is represented in a retelling by her suit-wearing, briefcase-carrying father, who, arriving home, confirms an earlier suspicion: "Fui y averigué. No está. Desapareció. Nadie sabe donde está. Mejor" (I went and asked. She not there. She disappeared. No one knows where she is. It's for the best). When asked how Lidia disappeared, the father is reluctant to explain and instead delegitimizes her: "Podés imaginarlo. A mí su vida me revuelve el estómago. Y no quiero cargar sobre mis espaldas lo que ella haga. Mejor. Lidia se murió" (You can imagine. Her lifestyle turns my stomach. And I don't want to bear the burden for what she does. It's for the best, Lidia died).

The father's reaction mimics the rhetoric employed in a societywide denial of the culpability of the dictatorship: "Expressions like 'it happened for a reason' and 'they must have done something' became popular to justify the kidnappings" (Novaro 154). Just as the father is blaming Lidia for her own disappearance, he slaps a mosquito on his neck, a gesture loaded with significance in a society in which much of the middle class supported the military's self-appointed mission to eliminate political militants as "subversives." He goes on to argue, "Lidia no debe olvidarse que es de una familia decente y dejarse arrastrar por un rufián bigotudo, aunque sea un profesor. . . . La debe tener en un prostíbulo" (Lidia mustn't forget that she comes from a decent family and not let herself be dragged around by a mustachioed pimp, even if he's a professor. . . . He must have her in a bordello).

This way of bringing Lidia's absence to light merits further discussion. Emilia's father attributes the disappearance to Lidia's own faulty decisions and a malevolent husband, but when this allegation is shown to be false, no other cause is alluded to. A very conspicuous will to silence is felt on the part of the characters—except Emilia, the only character willing to inquire about Lidia's absence—and of the film's narration, which shows the effects but omits the cause of her disappearance. Upon hearing her father's explanation, Emilia's own voice is heard in an interior monologue: "Así empezó todo. Y yo comprendí que tenía una misión que cumplir: buscar y encontrarla a mi hermana" (That's how it all started. And I understood I had a mission to carry out: to look for and find my sister). Emilia convinces her family to allow her to go to Buenos Aires to study, but her real motive is to investigate the fate of her sister.

As Emilia finds that the denials of knowledge spread to other characters, a consciousness of the *poder desaparecedor* starts to cohere the otherwise disparate elements of the story. These appear in episodes that appear to allude to further consequences of the kind of repressive actions that were being carried out by the state at the time of the film's making and viewing, yet these are repeatedly subject to claims of ignorance by different characters. As Calveiro writes of the effect that knowledge of the centers of detention had on society, "The concentration camps, that well-known secret that all fear, many disavow and quite a few deny, is only possible *when the totalizing intent by the state encounters its molecular expression*, submerges deeply in society, permeating it and nourishing itself from it" (1998, 28; italics in original). The effects of the *poder desaparecedor* on a wide variety of characters across society is reflected in their participation in denial in several ways.

As Emilia searches for her sister in the capital, on the back of a photo of Andrés she finds an address of the photo developing laboratory and goes there to inquire if they have any record of him. The clerk's immediate response is denial: "No, es imposible. De ninguna manera. No, ésta no está, ésta no aparece" (No, it's impossible. No way. No, this one's not here, this one won't appear). The response echoes the notorious public denial pronounced by General Videla when asked about the fate of those missing under the dictatorship: "Los desaparecidos no son, no están, no existen." Videla's denial makes clear his faith in the military's power to disappear not only individuals but also the representation of this power. Yet when Emilia insists, the clerk eventually agrees to look for the receipt, and he finds it. This long exchange, while forwarding the plot somewhat, makes more sense subtextually, as a veiled mise-en-scène of the searches for disappeared loved ones under the dictatorship and the denials they confronted.

In another episode, as Emilia surveils Andrés in a kind of cat-and-mouse game, they move through a crowd of people engrossed in watching a soccer match, thus oblivious to the presence of the two protagonists. In the year before the film's release, the World Cup was held in Argentina, and the national team won, an event that served the dictatorship as a distraction from human rights abuses and allowed it to gain support and continue the repression: "The organization in our country, in June 1978, of the World Cup and the victory for the Argentine team on the 25th of that month, were lived with a triumphalism encouraged from above, with the clear intention of distracting the population from its problems and blurring the image that the dictatorship had earned overseas" (Varea 77). These examples do not exhaust the allusions to the extracinematic actions of the dictatorship. Until recently, Andrés had worked as a professor, but no reason is given for why he no longer holds a post at the university. Although this severance goes unexplained, a cause is readily found in the reality outside the theater. The army's Operación Claridad (Operation clarity) was launched in 1977 to purge the nation of ideas that it saw as subverting "Occidental and Christian" values, as General Videla stated at the time. Professors deemed subversive were expelled from schools and universities, with many eliminated violently (Novaro 145). Operación Claridad could not be referenced in the cinema, especially not from a perspective in sympathy with a purged professor, but as an external interpretive key it answers yet another of the questions generated but left unanswered by the film.

The film also employs subjective sequences, both dream and waking, to represent inexplicable events and a nightmarish paranoia that obliquely reference the climate of fear of the time. In an interview at the time of the film's production, Landeck hints at how the film's representation of reality is refracted through the subjectivities of the characters: "I play with real facts seen through the characters. In some cases the vision is that of fantasy or imagination" (España 1977, 20). In one surprisingly explicit reference, Andrés walks along a sidewalk at night, oblivious to the presence of Emilia, who follows him. As thriller-film music is heard, suddenly a terrified young man runs the other way along the sidewalk, but no motivation for his flight is provided. Yet again, with this seemingly gratuitous event, the unspoken, unspeakable cause points to the military's *poder desaparecedor* and the practice of knowing-yet-denial it brought about, as the only explanation by which the film's narrative can make sense. In another dream of Emilia's, a narrative framing as subjective that might have been intended to sneak its content by the censors, Andrés is sleeping. He wakes up, agitated, runs to the window, and looks out to see a group of men below trying to force open the door to his building. He says to himself, "Estoy loco, este es un país civilizado. Estoy loco. Es un sueño, pero por la dudas . . ." (I'm crazy, this is a civilized country. I'm crazy. It's a dream, but just in case . . .). He picks up a club and positions himself just inside the door, ready to defend himself against the apparent *allanamiento*, thinking, "Esto no me está gustando. Mejor me acuesto y espero hasta que me despierte" (I'm not liking this at all. I'd better go to bed and wait until I awake up). Emilia's dream is apparently motivated by a consciousness of the *poder desaparecedor*, and the social reality of the dictatorship's *grupos de tarea* saturates the diegesis.

Though it has been left unexamined by critics and scholars, through its sustained creation of unsolved mysteries whose causes are absent in its diegesis yet readily attributable to state violence, with *Ese loco amor loco* Landeck found a strategy to represent, albeit indirectly, the violence of the dictatorship.[10] How could she do so in the shadow of the *poder desaparecedor*? Landeck's marginal position within the cultural field of the dictatorship is the key condition of the film's possibility. It was produced by Rumbo Producciones Cinematográficas, a company created for it by Landeck, Juan Legrin (Landeck's husband and coscriptwriter), Norberto Feldman, and Rubén Tarragona ("La directora Eva Landeck" 33). In an interview at the time, Landeck referenced the tight budget under which she worked: "The entire film will be made in exteriors . . . mine is an independent cinema, a cinema that cannot afford the luxury of filming 40,000 meters to only use 3,000" (1977, 20). As in the case of *Gente en Buenos Aires*, such a shoestring production model led to both freedom from commercial demands and, due to its unprotected position relative to the larger studios, difficulties with censorship and exhibition.

A comparison to the production of Landeck's earlier film is revealing of her responses to the different contexts. In *Gente en Buenos Aires*, a film made at a time of far more creative freedom and less state censorship and self-censorship, Landeck was able to represent an abduction, although the viewer is not given access to whatever information about its causes and perpetrators might be known by the film's protagonist, Pablo. But under the pressures of the dictatorship such a representation becomes impossible, and in *Ese loco amor loco* Landeck uses a far more restricted narration, one closer to the conventions of the detective genre. The focalizer is Emilia, and the story information supplied is usually restricted to that which is known to her, but since she is from a small town and immerses herself in literary texts, she is somewhat naive about social reality. But the film assumes a viewer far more aware than Emilia of the dictatorship's violence, one whose relatively abundant knowledge of the extratextual reality in which the film was made and viewed takes on importance. While Emilia does not complete a coming-of-age process of increasing awareness and never openly solves the enigma of Lidia's disappearance, this failure can be attributed to the impossibility of representing such an awareness under the dictatorship.

Ese loco amor loco was "prohibited for minors under the age of 18," a rating that amounts to an after-the-fact censorship that destroys a film's economic prospects, and the few press reviews of the film were negative. The conservative daily *La Nación* reflects the incoherence produced by a viewing of the film if the effects of the dictatorship's violence are willfully ignored: "Eva Landeck manages in some sequences to create an attractive climate of mystery and the film has moments of undeniable visual quality. But those positive aspects do not compensate for the general weakness of the narration that often becomes confused and suffers from a lack of precision and coherence in the dialogues" ("Fantasía y realidad"). Where a critical viewer of its time might have seen a coded indictment of the dictatorship's actions, the reviewer sees confusion and incoherence. Given such a review, it is no surprise that *Ese loco amor loco* performed badly at the box office and did not remain on-screen in Buenos Aires beyond its opening week.[11]

Landeck attests to earlier censorship of the script and other roadblocks presented by the dictatorship's functionaries: "It didn't turn out like I planned because I couldn't work with the actors for whom I had planned the script—because the authorities did not approve of them—and because they censored the script four times" (Trelles Plazaola 204–205).[12] In addition to the problem Landeck describes, that of the blacklisting of certain actors and other film professionals, a brief newspaper article on the shooting of the film reports the presence of the representatives of the *poder desparecedor* on set, in the form of the director and subsecretary of the Instituto Nacional de Cinematografía ("Eva Landeck inició"), commanders in the Argentine navy under Admiral Massera, who personally ran the notorious torture center at the Escuela Mecánica de la Armada. Such conspicuous presences on set point to official suspicions and a clear attempt at intimidation. Landeck references such official pressures when she attributes the censorship of the script of *Ese loco amor loco* to two factors specific to her case: the ill will on the part of the authorities she had generated with *Gente en Buenos Aires*, and her lack of the backing of an economically powerful production company: "That censorship made no sense, absolutely none at all, it was a bit of personal vengeance, the satisfaction of saying, 'since we didn't censor your first one, we'll censor this one.' But this film was clean, it didn't have anything censurable.... I think that if I had an important producer they wouldn't have dared do that" (Trelles Plazaola 205). Landeck's attribution of state censorship to her lack of alliance with the powerful studios alludes to the consequences of the celluloid ceiling on the creative freedom of those women who managed to direct by going outside established production models. Even in the 1970s, the larger production companies did not give women the opportunity to direct, and without the protection afforded by such patronage, the vengeful actions taken by the censors had a greater impact on Landeck's creative possibilities. She expands further on the treacherous intersection of gender, industry, and state power:

> At first my feminine condition wasn't an obstacle, quite the contrary. They behaved well with me, but, unfortunately, my first film was good, had success, won a prize and there the problem started. I suppose the same thing would have happened to a man, but more to me. All this is more serious when you're a woman. At first I didn't notice it: when I was this poor girl who got herself in too deep, who tried to make a film, everyone treated me marvelously and helped me. It wasn't only my condition as a woman but also the fact of not belonging to the group with money. (Trelles Plazaola 205)

Landeck posits that while her gender may have provided her with a temporary advantage due to the sympathy it generated, in the long term it proved a hindrance, since the economically powerful producers, less subject to the pressures of the state, did not readily employ women as directors. She never directed again in Argentina.

Landeck made her last feature film, *El lugar del humo*, in Uruguay in 1979, after she was contracted by a group of wealthy film students who felt they would benefit from working under an experienced director (Trelles Plazaola 206–207). The film, then, was made with yet another alternative production model, but this one forced Landeck to take extra care with references to the reality of Uruguay under the dictatorship. She recounts that the presence among the film students of a nephew of one of the members of the Uruguayan military junta forced her to self-censor during the filming itself, and she considers the result to be deeply flawed (Trelles Plazaola 204–205).

El lugar del humo employs an ensemble cast to narrate a bleak tour of an impoverished traveling theater company, and near its end it unpredictably transforms into a murder mystery. Like *Ese loco amor loco*, *El lugar del humo* contains ellipses and unexplained occurrences, but its subtexts are less elaborated. Yet despite the pressures to self-censor, Landeck's third film also manages to touch on the violence of the dictatorships. She mentions one sequence in particular, in which the characters gaze, horrified, out to the sealike river that separates Uruguay from Argentina: "There is a scene in which two actors were singing and suddenly they tense up with emotion as they look out on the river. It was because of the blood of the mutilated bodies of Argentines that floated over from the other shore. The relative of the [junta member] came over and asked me: 'What are they seeing?' I said 'dead fish.' He turned around and left. He couldn't say anything because there was nothing to see" (Hardouin and Ivachow 50). As in *Ese loco amor loco*, here the unrepresentable cause of the *poder desaparecedor* is elided: the practice of disposing of the corpses of victims in the Río de la Plata had been used since the first months of the Argentine dictatorship, and systematically since the middle of 1977 (Novaro 153).

Landeck engages more explicitly with censorship in a sequence in which a theater owner bans the company's play, saying, "Vea, no soy un censor, pero aplico mi opinión. Soy jurado, juez y legislador" (Look, I'm not a censor, but I apply my opinion. I'm jury, judge and legislator), then lays out his reasoning: "Está el caso de la chica esa que se va con el hombre y no se ve que están casados" (There's the case of that girl who leaves with the man and you don't show them as married). One of the actors responds: "¿Quiere que agreguemos alguna escena que haga referencia a que se casan?" (You want us to add a scene that refers to them getting married?).

The theater owner's reply, "pero tendría que ser por la iglesia y con velo blanco" (but it would have to be by the church and with a white veil), makes clear that this episode is a reference to the objections by the censor to Landeck's previous film, *Ese loco amor loco*, to which she referred in an interview:

> Tato asked me "How can it be that that girl and that guy go off together without getting married?" I told him: "That's the problem? The film is finished, I can't change it. What I can do, in a voice-over, is have him tell her they need to get married." I said that thinking about the producers. Tato was keeping an eye on me because of *Gente en Buenos Aires*. Then he said: "No, it has to be by the church and in white." After that he started laughing. He realized by himself that what he was saying was ridiculous. (Hardouin and Ivachow 50)

This representation of censorship as closely linked to economic power is incisive in the context of dictatorship-era cultural production. The prevalent mode of criticizing censorship was by representing it as an imposition on society by a kind of omnipotent being or monster whose origin in that society is ignored or, as Fernando Ramírez Llorens puts it, "the erasure of references to the groups that ideologically sustain and exert it" (2016, 16). As Ramírez Llorens writes, such contemporary representations were due to the immediate imperative to combat censorship, rather than understand it. En *El lugar del humo*, the censor is embedded as the owner of the theater itself, an individual who, in addition to sharing opinions and phobias with Tato, both clearly answers to the church and embodies the link between economic power and the control over exhibition.

El lugar del humo was clearly far more compromised by economic pressures and censorship than was *Gente en Buenos Aires*. In its currently available form, plot holes and discontinuities appear to confirm the censorship to which Landeck referred. She retired from filmmaking after this final experience, which she recounts as follows: "I finished the film and returned to Buenos Aires sick, really sick, because . . . technically the film was a disaster. . . . I was destroyed, with my health completely deteriorated. I said to myself, and my family repeated it to me: 'If you keep filming in those conditions it's because you're suicidal.' They made me realize that in order to film I needed to have normal conditions, and not film under special circumstances. The circumstances under which I had filmed were not normal conditions" (Trelles Plazaola 207–208). After this final film Landeck turned to occasional writing. She has published two novels—*Lejos de Hollywood* in 1995 and *Máscaras provisorias* in 2016—both with filmmaking themes, but has not returned to direction. Looking back on her career in film in a recent interview, she expressed regret: "I feel my career was frustrated, because they cut it off. I had many things to do still, to experience even. Well, I couldn't do it" (INCAA TV).

The increased presence of women as directors in Argentina in the last twenty years has generated much published scholarship but very little reexamination of the role of women as directors before Bemberg, which remains insufficiently understood. The uniqueness of Bemberg's case in Argentine cinema bears repeating. She faced censorship, such as when the original script of *Señora de nadie* (1982) "was turned down by the censors on the grounds that it set a bad example to housewives, since it was to be filmed by a woman, it dealt with adultery and also included a homosexual character" (King, 19). Her films continued to cause scandal due to their liberal stance on gender and their critique of the institution of marriage in the context of a conservative society, but Rita De Grandis makes the point that Bemberg's privileged origin also imposed certain blind spots on her work. She writes that the director's "notable artistic participation was made possible and at the same time limited by her origin and class perspective. . . . She was even naive enough to think that a woman who worked has certain advantages as far as freedom of self-affirmation at being obligated to earn a living" (4). De Grandis is not alone in recognizing Bemberg's failure to acknowledge the situation of, and difficulties faced by, women outside her own privileged class, of which the story of the directorial career of Landeck serves as an illuminating example.

In films produced under very marginal conditions, Landeck exposed her female (and male, for that matter) protagonists to complex social and economic pressures that affected all aspects of their existence. As a result, her films were suppressed, she withdrew from filmmaking, and the marginal status of her work effectively prevented it from entering into dialogue with that of subsequent generations.

Martha Lauzen conducts a yearly statistical analysis of the gender-based division of labor—the "celluloid ceiling"—in U.S. cinema. If such a study were to be carried out on Argentine cinema, it would no doubt find an improved situation in recent decades, but its quantitative approach would be blind to the vast differences between the production histories of the work of Bemberg and Landeck, the opportunities they enjoyed, and the difficulties they faced. A more incisive analysis would better account for the factors that resulted in Bemberg's filmmaking continuity, as well as the causes of the premature end of Landeck's directorial career. While Bemberg, despite getting a relatively late start as a director, achieved filmmaking continuity and made six feature films between 1980 and 1993, Landeck's politics, very problematic in the context of an authoritarian military regime, and her unprotected position at the margins of an industry closed to women directors led to the immediate suppression and mutilation of her work and the truncation of a promising directorial career.

3
Beauvoir before Bemberg

Though María Luisa Bemberg's feature films are often considered to be the inaugural feminist vision in the Argentine cinema, such a version of history neglects three women who made films earlier: Vlasta Lah, María Herminia Avellaneda, and María Elena Walsh. While Bemberg declared herself and her work to be feminist, these earlier filmmakers establish a different kind of relationship between their work and feminism, one closer to Andrea Giunta's characterization of artists who have not necessarily participated in a feminist movement or postulated a feminist art, but who "join in a critique of the dominant representations, which they seek to deconstruct and erode. Theirs is a feminist conscience that does not imply militancy in feminist organizations" (2018 84). Each of these filmmakers engages critically with dominant social constructions of gender in ways that, I argue, share a conscience of women's condition that could be most accurately called Beauvoirian.

The previous chapters described how established film producers had allowed little room for women in creative roles, but this gendered division also extended to film criticism and spectatorship. All aspects, that is, of cinema production and consumption were dominated by men, allowing very little room for women's creative participation. In order to understand the gendering of film production, consumption, and criticism in midcentury Argentine cinema, a passage from María Rosa Olivera-Williams on novelistic production in the midcentury and what she terms the "creation of the feminine" makes for a revealing comparison:

> The creation of the feminine as a focus of knowledge in novels written by women shows different perspectives on a world that was thought to be already known. Before the 1940s, few Latin American women managed to write novels. The fact that beginning in the decade of the 1950s an important number of women wrote novels in the Southern Cone underlines their need to ask questions about their feminine subjectivity. The question: Who are we as women?—at a moment in which silence and lack of political action around matters of gender and the apparent social acceptance of these quieted and made invisible the force of the women's movements that had fought for political and civil rights in the first half of the 20th century—motivated the creation of novels. (8–19)

While the invisibility described by Olivera-Williams motivated production in the 1950s of novels written by women who asked questions about gendered subjectivity and wrote about Argentine reality from perspectives that the wider culture was ignoring, in the less restricted field of production of the cinema this was not the case. In films of that decade, *lo femenino* had yet to be created, and the "different perspectives" were absent. The multiple forces of inertia of the field of cinema—commercial, critical, spectatorial, and syndical, to name a few—were apparently more resistant there than in the field of novelistic production, and women were mostly still restricted to certain hidden tasks in the Taylorized chain of production, leaving the question of feminine subjectivity unaddressed as women were largely limited to being objects of the spectatorial gaze.

In such a context, Vlasta Lah's two films of the early 1960s could be seen as an initial step toward a "creation of the feminine" in the cinema. But Lah's films, despite exploring such novel perspectives, failed to impact a cinematic field that was not yet prepared to receive them as it would Bemberg's work two decades later. The key condition that prepared the ground for Bemberg would come later, with the widespread cultural modernization of the 1960s and 1970s—which included the wider reception of second-wave feminism in Argentina, especially in the form of Simone de Beauvoir's work—that entered into a productive tension with socially conservative authoritarian politics.

Beauvoir's work was first translated into Spanish with the publication in 1947, in the review *Sur*, of the essay "Literatura y metafísica." The translation by María Rosa Oliver (cofounder of *Sur* with Victoria Ocampo) of "Littérature et métaphysique" appeared only a year after the original was published in *Les Temps Modernes*. Beauvoir's landmark *Le deuxième sexe* was initially put into print in France in 1949, and its first translation into Spanish, as *El segundo sexo*, appeared in 1954 in Argentina (Ediciones Psique, in a version by Pablo Palant) (Smaldone 395–398). The translation of *Pour une morale de l'ambiguïté* into Spanish as *Para una moral de la ambigüedad* (1956 in Editorial Schapire) soon followed.[1] Despite these early publications and the strong presence of Sartrean existentialism in the 1950s (particularly evident in the journal *Contorno*, published from 1953 to 1959), the reaction to Beauvoir in the 1950s was minimal in Argentina (Tarducci; Nari 70).

Mónica Tarducci's research into the reception of *The Second Sex* in Argentina encounters this lack of resonance of Beauvoir's work in the cultural field of the 1950s. She narrates her investigation in the first person: "To make contact with women who had read *The Second Sex* before the decade of the sixties was a difficult challenge. The immense majority had read it near the end of that decade or in the seventies. . . . Through deep personal involvement between the interviewees and myself, we managed to convince ourselves that if indeed, during the fifties not much happened, it was a period of latency, a preparation for the sixties, which meant in some cases to be able to make the big jump toward the feminism of the seventies" (130). Like Tarducci, Marcela Nari describes a gradual awakening of a feminist consciousness in Argentina. She writes that in the 1970s *The Second Sex* was accorded an importance retrospectively by a new feminist consciousness, one that was not there to receive it in the 1950s and 1960s. Referring to her own search, Nari writes that in the 1950s "references to *The Second Sex* do not abound and, when they appear, are rather about distant readings among other readings, and which valorize aspects of the book (objectivity, for example) that many years later, in memories, will not appear as the most relevant" (71). While the wider reception of Beauvoir happened gradually, there was, nonetheless, a core of Argentine women writers in whose work Beauvoir's influence was clearly felt before 1970, the most often mentioned being Silvina Bullrich (who translated several of Beauvoir's books into Spanish), Marta Lynch, Silvina Ocampo, Salvadora Medina Onrubia, Emma Barrandéguy, Beatriz Guido, Alejandra Pizarnik, Aurora Venturini, and Sara Gallardo (André 108; Smaldone 412). This list suggests that Beauvoir's direct impact was mostly felt in a cultural field that, although it produced some best sellers, was still decidedly more restricted than that of a commercial cinema that was always slow to incorporate new ideas that might alienate certain sectors of its much-needed paying public.

The first appearance of *The Second Sex* in the Argentine cinema is often attributed to the presence of the book itself in the diegesis of *Crónica de una señora*, the 1970 film scripted by Bemberg and directed by Raúl de la Torre, in which the wealthy protagonist, Fina, played by Graciela Borges, reads the book in the French original and subsequently awakens to a consciousness of her subordinated condition as a woman. This appearance underlines the exclusivity associated with Beauvoir's work in terms of class and language, an exclusivity that may have contributed to the failure of Lah's *Las furias* to be received as a feminist text in a popular national medium that in 1960 had a limited viewership among Argentina's Francophile economic elites.[2]

The importance of Beauvoir's work in the rapid growth of Argentine feminism in the 1970s is widely noted. Among many others, Bemberg nodded to her frequently in both films and interviews, recounting in one of the latter an experience similar to that of the protagonist of *Crónica de una señora*: "Since childhood I had felt a sense of frustration, a double standard between my brothers and me. This was a rebellion I had had since being a girl, and it manifested itself especially after reading Simone de Beauvoir's *Second Sex*, which was like an explosion in the mind of the majority of women of my age. I will never be able to adequately express my appreciation for that book. It was like a dam that burst" (André 111). Bemberg cofounded the Unión Feminista Argentina (UFA) in 1970 and during that decade wrote the scripts for the feature-length narrative films *Crónica de una señora* and *Triángulo de cuatro* (Fernando Ayala, 1975) and directed the militant feminist short films *El mundo de la mujer* (1972) and *Juguetes* (1978), then *Momentos* (1980), the first of a string of very widely seen features for which she is generally considered Argentina's first feminist filmmaker.

Bemberg's films were groundbreaking in the national context not only for their commercial success and awards but also for their representation of female characters, which André describes in terms that clearly echo Beauvoir's work:

> Previous representations of women both in literature and films produced by men . . . mostly depicted female characters who ascribe to traditional phallocratic perceptions of love, in which a woman is only considered complete through her total surrender or subjection to a man and the masculine subject grants transcendence to the feminine objectified Other. Bemberg's productions constantly subvert and deconstruct romantic or hegemonic visions of the feminine in favor of more autonomous and independent gender relations in which women either refuse to be the Other to the male subject or embrace their alterity without falling victim to hierarchical subordinations. (André 113)

Although this is certainly an accurate account of how gender relations play out both in the national cinema tradition and in Bemberg's reconfiguration of it, I would argue that she was not the first Argentine filmmaker to integrate a Beauvoirian conception of women's condition into her work. Two decades before Bemberg's first feature-length film, Lah directed *Las furias* and *Las modelos*, films that engage with gendered embodied existence and the relational nature of freedom, through a unique attentiveness to the tension between women's possible resistance to subordination and the limitations imposed by the particular facticity of the films' Argentine settings. But they did so at a time when the Argentine cultural field appears to have generally lacked the specific competence needed to engage with the films in these terms. While the female characters in *Las furias* are exemplary, in both positive and negative ways, of Beauvoirian ethics as expressed in *The Ethics of Ambiguity* and *The Second Sex*, neither audiences nor critics appear to have been sufficiently competent in Beauvoir's ideas to have perceived the films' gender politics in such terms. Had they been, *Las furias* might have entered Argentine film history as the initial engagement with women's condition through the perspectives of women, and Lah's grappling with issues of gendered existence and the stark choices faced by women would have been recognized.

Las furias premiered on November 3, 1960, nearly four decades after the previous film directed by a woman in Argentina. Perhaps it is no coincidence that the first woman to challenge the celluloid ceiling was an immigrant. While the little biographical information published on Lah is contradictory, it is agreed that she is from an area near the border between Italy and Yugoslavia.[3] She had the opportunity, unavailable for women at the midcentury in Argentina, to study filmmaking, doing so at the Scuola Nazionale di Cinematografia (later more famous as the Centro Sperimentale), and also studied theater at the Accademia Nazionale d'Arte Drammatica.[4] In Argentina she worked often as assistant director, beginning in the late 1930s, and was director of the short-lived Escuela Cinematográfica Argentina de la Unidad Básica Cultural Eva Perón, founded in 1954 and dedicated "the training of artists and technicians" to work in the national cinema ("Se ha Fundado" 178). According to the limited information available, it operated in downtown Buenos Aires and offered classes at night and on Saturday mornings; its professors were industry figures, mostly men, although women taught in the roles in which they tended to work in the industry, such as wardrobe, voice, and dance.[5] Based on the very limited information I have found, it is not clear if the students were exclusively women, or if men participated as well. The school appears to have functioned for only a few months, from June 1955 until the coup in September of that year ("Noticioso" 122).[6]

The story of Lah's professional career in the Argentine studios serves as an example of a woman's condition worthy of *The Second Sex*. For more than two decades, beginning in the late 1930s, she worked in Argentina as assistant director to her husband, Catrano Catrani, and other directors on at least nineteen films, before a brief experience as director of two films (D. López 66–67). Mariana Inés Conde notes that Lah's case is paradigmatic of the situation of women working in cinema at that time, since she "had few opportunities in a highly productive, low-cost market, for which she was intellectually and technically prepared. It was not, then, a matter of risking the business in the hands of an untrained person" (2009, 188–189). Lah herself, when asked in an interview why she had not yet directed after working for so many years as an assistant, attributed it to her gender: "Because I'm a woman. If not, I'd have been filming for the last ten years. For ten years I've been capable of doing it" ("Por primera vez" n. pag.). While it was surely uncommon for women to be trained in direction in Argentina, since there were literally no prospects for working in that capacity, despite her professional formation and extensive experience Lah was able to direct only twice during a long career in the industry. But my interest in her films goes beyond the mere fact of the gender of their director.

If considered in the context of the Argentine cinema field of the early 1960s, her two films treat gender in radical ways. But they were reviewed infrequently and negatively, and despite being the first films directed by a woman in forty years, they could accurately be called a nonevent in Argentine film historiography. Copies exist today (they were screened in 2016 at the Mar del Plata Film Festival and at the Museo de Arte Latinoamericano de Buenos Aires), but the films are seldom seen and have been difficult to find even in digital format.[7] Very little has been written about them and their director, and much of this has been dismissive, often in stubbornly gendered terms, of which Daniel López's entry in the catalog of the 2016 Mar del Plata Festival serves as an example.

López first reports the opinion of a male colleague of Lah in terms that avoid referencing her professional capacities in favor of a return to qualities that recall the notion of the Eternal Feminine— "he remembered her affectionately as a very good woman, with whom the day-to-day filming was pleasant, especially due to her sharp sense of humor" (64–65)—before directly quoting his opinion that "she was as skinny and ugly as a sardine" (65). López compounds the colleague's failure to address Lah's professional capacity by dismissing her direction of *Las furias* with a claim that it is more worthwhile to pay attention to Astor Piazzolla's music and the acting of the female cast (65). His critical vision combines an approval of the presence of women in a more proper place, in front of the camera, with a willful neglect of Lah's more creative role, a vision further confirmed in his account of her second film, *Las modelos*, whose "heroines are played justly by professional models, splendid women and not such bad actresses as one might expect" (66).

Other critics have dismissed *Las furias* as *teatro filmado* (filmed theater) (Manrupe and Portela 242) or *melodrama desatado* (wild melodrama) (Maranghello 159), while Fernando Martín Peña's brief but more considered evaluation of the film puts it in a list of "failed yet interesting titles" (2012, 173). Yet a closer look at the film reveals it to be an original and incisive engagement with women's condition, and thus a key yet forgotten film of a moment of creative flourishing in Argentine cinema.

By the late 1950s the Argentine studio system had entered into a crisis from which it would never recover, and a new way of making films was already becoming established by the more independent filmmakers who would be known as the Generación del 60. Although this generation signaled the full arrival of cinematic modernity in Argentina, it was as bereft of female directors as were the studios, as Lah is not considered part of it. *Las furias* was produced at Lumiton Studios, where Lah had worked in other capacities on more than two dozen films, and its production was more in a remnant industrial than an independent mode (Fabbro 242–243). Instead of the location shooting more typical of the new generation, the mansion in which most of the action takes place was built as a set, as Lah described in an interview conducted during the film's production: "We built the entire house, two floors. Below is the dining room, the great hall, the study, the kitchen. Above, the four bedrooms. Each is furnished and decorated according to a distinct time and psychology, according to its inhabitant" ("Se reúnen las furias" 4). Despite the formidable production investment Lah describes, Gabriela Fabbro accounts for the film's shortcomings as symptomatic of the decline of the studio: "Upon analyzing only the final productions of Lumiton, *Codicia* (1955, Catrani), *Reportaje en el infierno* (1959, Viñoly Barreto) and *Las furias* (1960, Vlasta Lah), the steady fall becomes evident. Inferior productions, with dialogue full of rhetoric and commonplaces. The studio was losing its way. It tried to find it in new faces (but not for that new aesthetic directions), with Vlasta Lah (wife of Catrano Catrani), who in two films tried to take on the task of direction, with unhappy results" (243). While Fabbro sees in *Las furias* only evidence of Lumiton's decline, attention to the film within its greater cultural context reveals an early, formally inventive exploration, from a woman's perspective, of gender and the traditional limitations imposed on women. The film engages directly with the dilemma central to *The Second Sex*, that of woman's condition as defined by the conflict between freedom and the facticity specific to her situation. In doing so, it thematizes questions much like those with which Beauvoir closes the introduction to *The Second Sex*: "How, in the feminine condition, can a human being accomplish herself? What paths are open to her? Which ones lead to dead ends? How can she find independence within dependence? What circumstances limit women's freedom and how can she overcome them?" (16–17). While today's spectator might be inclined to criticize Lah's films for not providing a positive model of liberation, I argue that if such anachronistic expectations are avoided it becomes clear that the films formulate critical explorations of women's condition resonant with those found in Beauvoir's *The Ethics of Ambiguity* and *The*

Second Sex, both of which had been translated and published in Argentina in the previous decade. Lah herself discusses the characters in terms that reflect Beauvoir's writings on women's situation and her proposed ethics of reciprocity: "They're not bad. It's that they find themselves surrounded by adverse circumstances. Everything is hostile to them. None knows how to overcome and try to improve the life of that home that is a hell. Each one lives consumed by her interior drama and unable to find a helping hand that might help her to escape it" ("Se reúnen las furias" 4). Lah's description of the condition of her characters reads like a popularization of Beauvoir's feminist existentialism and ethics of reciprocity. In the interest of examining the films in their own modernity, within, that is, the terms emergent in the cultural field of their time, I will employ Beauvoir's early texts as an interpretive key.

Lah's debut film's representation of women and female desire is surprisingly modern, despite certain other aspects of *Las furias* being ponderously conventional, particularly the declamatory dialogue and the at-times excessively theatrical acting. While the film is an adaptation of the 1950 play of the same name by Enrique Suárez de Deza, Lah is credited with both adaptation and direction, and thus appears to have played the central authorial role in the filmic version. Her second and last film is *Las modelos*, first screened in 1963, on which she shares scriptwriting credits with Abelardo Arias, the writer and cofounder, in 1957, of Editorial Tirso, the first local publishing house to specialize in gay fiction.[8] In addition to its exploration of the existential situation of its female characters, whose perspectives on relationships are the film's central concern, *Las modelos* contains one of the first depictions of the situation of a gay character in Argentina's homonegative culture of the time, a daring choice within the popular medium of the cinema.[9] Lah's films are among the first, and indeed the very first from a female auteur in Argentine sound cinema, in which female characters focalize the narration and narrative events are motivated by female desire.[10] In these utterly novel representations of female perspective and subjectivity lies Lah's most intriguing, yet unrecognized, contribution to Argentine cinema.

Before turning to Lah's films, a final point must be made regarding some of the differences between the philosophical writings of Beauvoir and those of Jean-Paul Sartre, so as to make clear how Lah's films incorporate Beauvoir's unique ideas on the situatedness of freedom, despite Sartre's wider reception in Argentina in the 1950s. For the Beauvoir of *The Ethics of Ambiguity* and *The Second Sex*, freedom is not radical, but deeply situated in a social context and conditioned by interpersonal relations. Beauvoir calls the subject to self-conscious engagement with the world through actions that both manifest the subject's freedom and, importantly, encourage the freedom of others, enabling a transcendence of the given (or "factical") situation that includes the oppression of others. In *The Second Sex*, Beauvoir posits this ethic in terms of the relationship between female and male, arguing that the link between the sexes has been an extreme expression—one so persistent that it is quasi-ahistorical—of a Hegelian primordial dynamic of struggle and domination between subject and other, in which man affirms his subject position by acting in the social sphere through work, politics, and intellectual life, and in the private sphere by subordinating women. Women are thus mired in an immanence that men are able to transcend.

Sonia Kruks addresses the differences between Beauvoir and Sartre regarding their conceptualizations of situation. She points out that Beauvoir's philosophy has often been considered derivative of Sartre's, in part due to Beauvoir's self-positioning as such, but she argues that Beauvoir's ideas present formidable challenges to those of Sartre: "This is particularly the case with her treatment of the question of the situated nature of subjectivity. In *The Second Sex* especially, she came to conclusions ... which were clearly opposed to Sartre's account, in *Being and Nothingness*, of the autonomy of the subject" (Kruks 84). This opposition to Sartre's account of autonomy centers on the importance of situation in limiting individual freedom and on intersubjectivity. Focusing her analysis on the same early texts that had been translated and published in Buenos Aires, *The Ethics of Ambiguity* and *The Second Sex*, Kruks argues that while for the Sartre of the time interpersonal relationships could only be characterized as conflictive, Beauvoir counters by exploring the possibility of relationships of reciprocal generosity and how these might form projects that create a future open to the transcendence of the factic. As Kruks writes, "Beauvoir raises the startling possibility that a *common situation* can give rise to a *common project*—in other words that a joint action is what creates ensembles" (94). These common projects, called "we-projects" by Debra Bergoffen, can range in scope from the reciprocity possible within a couple to larger collective movements. This is where *The Second Sex*'s project itself opens onto the future and to feminism as a movement. In Lah's films, not only is the situation examined that of women, but the possibility of the common project as a couple is central, as is the stubborn resistance of facticity in the face of transformative action.

Four of the five female protagonists of *Las furias* are, in the terms of Beauvoir's ethics, represented as mired in immanence. Unreflective consumers of culture-industry products marketed to women, they fully accept their factic subordination and conform to the sort of social construction of femininity that Beauvoir describes. The film, then, appears to share in Beauvoir's postulation that the stereotypical differences between men and women emerge from systematic situational differences, and it is difficult to avoid seeing in the final female character, the *amante* (the lover, played Olga Zubarry), a positively inflected embodiment of the ethical propositions contained in Beauvoir's description of women who strive to overcome the socially constructed feminine condition. As she writes near the end of *The Second Sex*, in the chapter entitled "The Independent Woman": "There are quite a lot of privileged women today who have gained economic and social autonomy in their professions. They are the ones who are at issue when the question of women's possibilities and their future is raised" (723).[11] The *amante* is a business owner who has achieved economic autonomy by working outside the home, who prides herself on her ability to act on equal terms with men. Instead of defining herself relative to a man as *other*, she is an independent woman who has taken consciousness of her condition, chosen her own destiny, and constructed a relationship of reciprocity with a man, thus seeking to transcend the factical by encouraging both her and his freedom. Lah's casting against type of Olga Zubarry in this role needs to be mentioned. Zubarry was usually cast in roles that emphasized her physical attractiveness, often as victimized characters. In *Las furias* her sexuality is minimized by a wardrobe of business suits and thick-framed glasses. By introducing such a character to the Argentine cinema and casting Zubarry in the role, Lah joins in Beauvoir's project to "make visible the myths of femininity written by laborious masculine hands" and challenge these by writing "other 'myths' outside the myth of alterity, outside of the beautiful tyranny of the feminine," as Alejandra Castillo describes the philosopher's project (48–49).

In contrast to the *amante*, the other four female protagonists are clearly the furies of the title. In the laborious male hands of Greek mythology, the Furies are vengeful goddesses who punish certain crimes "by hounding the culprits relentlessly, without rest or pause [until] their victims die in torment" (Graves 122). These four all belong to a single wealthy, decadent family and are portrayed as suffering from many of the conditions Beauvoir considers proper to unemancipated women's existence. Assiduous and unreflexive consumers of mass culture marketed to women—romantic films, *radionovelas*, and fashion magazines—that transparently mediates their desires, the condition of each is primarily determined by her relationship to the absent male character, Marcelo. He is seldom at home, since he works and often spends the night at the apartment of the *amante*, and is only briefly glimpsed in the film, as he leaves the house in the morning. Yet despite his absence he provides an essential centering presence for this domestic universe of subordinated females, although it is later revealed that only within the mansion is he of such importance, since in society his professional and economic status is mediocre at best. Each of the furies is named according to her relationship with him: the *madre* (the mother, played by Mecha Ortiz) is the smothering matriarch who dotes on her son and ignores her daughter; the *esposa* (the wife, Aída Luz) is determined to preserve her loveless marriage at all costs; the *hermana* (the sister, Alba Mugica) is a forty-something *solterona* (spinster) whose education was sacrificed in favor of her brother's; and the *hija* (the daughter, Elsa Daniel) is resolutely cynical despite her youth, her only ambition being that of using marriage to escape the stifling home. The furies, who constantly bicker and inflict microaggressions on each other, fit Beauvoir's description of woman subordinated to a man and condemned to domestic immanence: "Since he is producer, it is he who goes beyond family interest to the interest of society and who opens a future to her by cooperating in the construction of the collective future: it is he who embodies transcendence. Woman is destined to maintain the species and care for the home, which is to say, to immanence" (*The Second Sex* 443). In Marcelo's absence the home is very much what Beauvoir calls the *gynaceum*, an all-female space whose inhabitants "bask in contingency, in blandness, in boredom" (*The Second Sex* 588). For Beauvoir, the vast majority of women conform to this condition, which she sees as emerging not from biology but from the systematic situational difference between the sexes. Her further description of the resulting condition could also serve well as a description of the furies: "Enclosed in her flesh, in her home, she grasps herself as a passive opposite to these human-faced gods who set goals and standards. In this sense there is truth in the saying that condemns her to remaining 'an eternal child'. . . . She has no grasp, even in thought, on this *reality that involves her*. It is an opaque presence in her eyes" (*The Second Sex* 639; emphasis added). This reality that "involves," or, as alternative translations of "cette réalité qui l'investit," "surrounds" or "envelops" her, constitutes for Beauvoir the situation of women who fail to recognize their subordinate condition and take responsibility for their freedom. Even those who do achieve a degree of consciousness of the workings of this enveloping reality tend to fall into bad faith, convinced that they are better off rejecting their freedom than embracing it. This functions as an accurate description of the reality of the furies in the film, as well as, it appears, those in the 1950 source play, *Las furias* by Enrique Suárez de Deza, but in the case of the *amante*, the sole female character to temporarily transcend these conditions, the question of Lah's authorship must be addressed.

A comparison of the filmic adaptation with the text of Suárez de Deza's play would definitively answer questions about the extent of Lah's creative role, but despite an extensive search, I have been unable to locate that text.[12] Reviews of the play published at the time, however, do suggest significant alterations to the original by Lah, primarily having to do with the *amante* character. An anonymous reviewer of the play in *La Nación* on March 9, 1950, states that "the lover . . . only appears at the end, to announce the sudden death of the man on the desk at his office, and blames each of them for his failure and destruction, and recognizes her own involuntary blame" ("'Las furias' es una obra" 8). In Lah's filmic adaptation as well, the *amante* appears at the end to announce the man's death, but she is also present in an earlier sequence, in which the *madre* visits her in her office, where their conversation makes explicit the *amante*'s Beauvoir-like worldview. This central episode, presumably a creation of Lah's, is key for its character exposition of the *amante* as having overcome women's condition and for putting her ethical position in stark contrast with those of the furies.

The *amante* performs modern, liberated femininity during the conversation by gamely pulling a lighter out of a pocket on her dress and smoking a cigarette. She offers one to the *madre*, who declines, opting for a more gender-appropriate cup of tea. When the *madre* asks, "¿Ud. lo quiere mucho, verdad?" (You love him a lot, do you not?), the *amante* replies with an insistence on the kind of mutual recognition that Beauvoir might see as constitutive of a situated ethics of reciprocity: "*Nos* queremos mucho" (We love *each other* a lot). Then, when asked "¿A qué se dedica Ud.?" (What do you do?), the *amante* lays out a personal history and philosophy that reflect her dissatisfaction with that which makes up factic immanence for women, as well as a strong will to overcome it: "A los negocios. Viví solamente tres años con mi marido . . . mi casamiento no fue muy feliz. Mi marido y yo nos separamos de común acuerdo. Después del divorcio me dediqué al trabajo" (I'm in business. I only lived three years with my husband . . . my marriage was not very happy. My husband and I separated by mutual agreement. After the divorce I went to work). In addition to an attitude toward relationships that reflects a Beauvoirian ethics—"Only the freedom of others keeps each one of us from hardening in the absurdity of facticity" (*The Ethics of Ambiguity* 77)—the *amante*'s reference to her marital situation is particularly relevant in Argentina, where divorce laws were restrictive and politicized.[13] Here the *amante*'s attitude contrasts clearly with the bad faith of the *esposa*, who stubbornly refuses to grant Marcelo the freedom implied by a separation and thus fails to liberate herself. In addition to laying out these contrasts between the *amante* and the furies, this conversation serves as a link to another aspect of Beauvoir's critique of women's condition, that of the mediation of women's desires by mass culture.

When the mother admiringly acknowledges the other woman's abilities by saying "Debe ser Ud. una mujer muy hábil" (You must be a very capable woman), the *amante* responds with a Beauvoir-like declaration on gender relations: "Me defiendo. La vida de hoy exige que la mujer encuentre su independencia. Odio a las mujeres que le esperan todo del hombre" (I manage. In today's world a woman must find her own independence. I hate women who expect everything from a man). This closing declaration of the conversation is followed by an abrupt cut that puts the *amante*'s words in contact with the final sequence of a romantic movie seen projected on a screen, which is then eyeline matched to the teary-eyed *hermana* in the audience of the theater. The resulting association articulates a contrast in which the *hermana* serves as an example of the kind of woman both Beauvoir—who wrote of the "older woman's tragedy," in which, through a lifetime of immanence, a woman "realizes she is useless; all through her life, the bourgeois woman often has to resolve the derisory problem: How to kill time?" (*The Second Sex* 633)—and the *amante* disdain, as a naive consumer of the women's film, a genre "addressed to women in their traditional status under patriarchy—as wives, mothers, abandoned lovers . . ." (Williams 4). The woman's film conventionally suggests that only through a normative relationship with a man can a woman achieve fulfillment and feel complete.

The cinematic mediation of the *hermana*'s desire exemplifies the function in *Las furias* of culture-industry products in maintaining women in immanence. As Barbara S. Andrew writes, for Beauvoir "women's psychology, education and desire are so shaped by social influences that they learn to choose against themselves" (37). The cultural objects that mediate the desires of the furies are the conspicuously present magazines, radio programs, and films directed at a female consumer, and the mediation itself is represented as a somewhat mechanical process, in the form of actions that immediately follow imperatives. The *esposa*, who seldom leaves the house, listens to a radio serial called *El camino hacia la felicidad* (The road to happiness), in which the female character is heard to say to a man, "No me agrada pensar, me agrada oírte" (I don't like to think, I like to listen to you). When an advertising jingle interrupts the narration to urge that its listener "¡Tome café colombiano!" (Drink Colombian coffee!), the *hermana* overhears it and responds automatically to the prompt, asking "¿Hay café? ¡O sí, qué suerte!" (Is there any coffee? Oh, great, what luck!). She also reads the women's magazine *Vea y Lea*, where an advertisement for shoes on the back cover reproduces an imperative of inviolability of the heterosexual couple, reading "¡Ni con palanca se separan!" (Not even a crowbar can pry them apart!). The many culture-industry products seen or heard affirm a domesticity in which consumer goods provide consolation for the life of immanence of a woman unable to venture into society, while obliquely pointing to the themes, inseparable here, of divorce and sexuality, which will be central to the film's climax.

To counter such conditions, Beauvoir argues for a relational, intersubjective ethics, positing that ethical relationships demand projects undertaken in common, in which the individual puts the certainty of the self at risk in favor of a commitment to a "we" that Debra Bergoffen defines as "an intersubjectivity of allies where each one validates the other as its equal" (132). The ethicality of such projects lies in their conditioning the possibility of transcendence of the factic. Beauvoir extends this ethics to the realm of sexuality, on which she elaborates further in the 1951 *Faut-il brûler Sade?* In the writings and life of the Marquis de Sade, Beauvoir sees a sexuality that can never lead to transcendence, since, as she writes, "never . . . does sensual pleasure appear as self-forgetfulness, swooning, or abandon . . . he never, for an instant, loses himself in his animal nature; he remains so lucid, so cerebral, that philosophical discourse, far from dampening his ardor, acts as an aphrodisiac" (qtd. in J. Butler 184–185). Under the rigors of such a lucid lack of intoxication, the boundaries of the self can never give way to allow an apprehension of the presence of the other; they never open up to the "dangers of an eroticism willing to expose itself to the uncanny otherness of another's freedom" (Bergoffen 134). As such, Sade's sexuality can be neither reciprocal nor transformative in the way Beauvoir calls for. A parallel dynamic plays out in *Las furias*.

With only one of its female protagonists, the *amante*, existing actively outside the domestic world, the film attends closely to the private sphere of interpersonal relationships and sex, which the furies instrumentalize in purely self-interested ways and, as a result, fail to cultivate the freedom of their partners and a possible transcendence of facticity through what Bergoffen calls a "we-project" (133). Each fails to do so in her own specific way. The *esposa* insists on preserving her ruined marriage and the conjugal bed she shares infrequently and coldly with her husband, while the *hija* preserves her virginity because, as she states, "Quiero casarme, irme de esta casa. Si me entrego antes, el noviazgo sería muy largo, y no me conviene" (I want to get married, to get out of this house. If I give myself to him first, the courtship will be very long, and that doesn't suit me). She is convinced that her wealthy boyfriend's desire for sex will drive him to marry her sooner and take her away from the stifling home, in a radically individualistic project that seeks to create a couple that is not at all a we-project. The *hermana*, whose subordination to Marcelo has caused her a lifetime of frustration and dissatisfaction, had earlier that day seen the romantic movie that ended with a passionate kiss, which apparently perturbed her to such an extent that she sets out to lose her virginity. She first turns to autoerotic fantasy, then to a desire-driven sortie into the night, where she is taken for a prostitute and laughed at, apparently due to the incongruence between the showy dress she wears, her age, and her awkward attempts to flirt. This humiliation in turn drives her to move beyond sexual fantasy, into physical contact, but in this contact she fails to recognize the freedom of the other, in an episode to which I will return. These actions on the part of these three furies invite a reading of relationships and sexuality in the film in terms of Beauvoirian ethics, since none moves beyond self-serving action into an engagement with the other's freedom and the transcendence made possible by a commitment to a shared freedom and an open future.

A further discussion of the episode of the *hermana* will illustrate this dynamic. After the romantic film ends, she returns home. It can be assumed that she was perturbed by the film, likely by comparing the female character's blissful romance with her own middle-aged solitude. When she is met at the front gate with the delivery of a new dress ordered by the *hija*, she accepts it, but instead of giving it to her niece, she waits until the others are asleep, pours herself a drink, tries on the dress, and gazes at herself in a full-length mirror, which drives her to fantasize and beckon to the spectator to make love to her. Here the film goes beyond formal convention to mount a radical confrontation and redirection of what has often been held to be a male-gendered spectatorial gaze of the midcentury cinema. The young, attractive daughter played by Elsa Daniel (aged twenty-four at the time) had been seen earlier in the film in several shots wearing lingerie, a garter belt, and stockings, classic vestments of an object of scopophilia—the voyeuristic consumption of passive young women in beautiful clothing—accompanied by a tropicalized tango by Astor Piazzolla. But here she is substituted as object of the gaze by her stern, middle-aged spinster aunt, played by Alba Mugica, a character actor who tended to play decidedly unsexy roles. The crosscut sequence narrates in parallel the *hermana*'s fantasy and the *hija*'s night out on a date, which allows the latter to also serve as a representation of the former, in a dynamic that will radically reconfigure both Mugica's typecasting and the conventions through which the cinema addressed its spectator.

Gendered as male according to the models of apparatus theory elaborated by Laura Mulvey and other critics, the spectator is conventionally prompted to scopophilia. For the purposes of this analysis, it will be useful to further unpack this relationship of voyeurism and the film-viewing experience. As Damon Young writes, discussing Freud, "voyeurism is . . . a mode of relating to the object predicated on *distance*: it does *not* reach the object, which retains its separateness and thus its autonomy; voyeurism is *not* driven by a desire to 'have' the object; on the contrary, such 'having' would close the gap on whose preservation it depends" (43; emphasis in original). In *Las furias* this distance between spectator and object is overcome not by the young starlet Elsa Daniel (who had been the object of the voyeuristic gaze minutes before as she ambled through the house in lingerie) but by Alba Mugica, no longer a young woman but masquerading as such by wearing the younger woman's dress. The *hermana* takes an active role in her fantasized sex act, when, already in close-up, the camera tracks even further forward, into a kiss, after which, still in closeup, she takes a drink and gazes back at the viewer imploringly as the camera positions him to make love with her. The viewer, trapped in what apparatus theory calls primary identification, "an identification with the looking position constructed by the camera" (Young 28), is obligated to virtually make love with the *hermana*. This use of a subjective shot that corresponds to no diegetic character suspends the operation of secondary identification—identification with a diegetic character, or "screen surrogate" (28)—thus disrupting the usual, voyeuristic ontological conditions of the cinema, which "correspond to the spectator's invisibility in relation to the world viewed" (42). Instead of the usual nonreversibility of fiction-film address, the look is reversed by the *hermana*'s gaze into the camera, and the spectator is forced to renounce his mastery over the image. Immobilized in the theater seat, a conflict is sparked when, as Linda Williams describes of the "body genres," the film elicits a bodily response, and the viewer's flesh, willing or not, is summoned to action. But Lah's film soon goes further, when this process of mediating spectatorial desire and satisfying it only through a bait-and-switch is doubled within the diegesis of the film.

The spell of the *hermana*'s subjective fantasy is suddenly broken when she looks up and sees a photo portrait of the *madre* on the wall. Her mother had sacrificed the *hermana*'s future in the interest of that of her brother, to the point of discouraging her from marrying, and she remains a virgin. Still perturbed, but now firmly decided on freeing herself from the imposition of lifelong chastity, she decides to venture out wearing the new dress. In the street one man attempts to engage her from a car, assuming she is a prostitute; then several young men walking by stop to inspect her, only to reject her laughingly as one says, "¡Es una vieja, vámonos!" (She's an old lady, let's get out of here!). Flustered and frustrated, she hurries home, where she witnesses the *hija*'s drunken boyfriend (played by Guillermo Bredeston) drop her off at the front door. The young couple kisses, but the *hija*, intent on preserving her virginity so that the boyfriend will marry her as soon as possible in order to satisfy his sexual desire, refuses his drunken advances. Seeing this, the *hermana* hurries to the front gate, where the two parallel narrative lines converge. She intercepts the boyfriend, kisses him, and invites him to her room. The sexually frustrated younger man accepts the invitation, offering the justification, "¡La chica me tiene loco, me tiene loco!" (The girl's got me crazy, she's got me crazy!), and they make love.

This diegetic play of substitution of the boyfriend's object of desire repeats that imposed on the spectator, whose desire was sparked for the daughter but who instead made virtual love to her aunt. But where the diegetic boyfriend is drunk and thus less conscious of the bait-and-switch, the spectator, locked securely into primary identification, experiences the incident under no such intoxicant, with lucidity intact, conscious of the first-person experience and acutely aware of the lack of freedom as he is subjected to the *hermana*'s solipsistic eroticism. A more powerful cinematic illustration of the desirability of a Beauvoirian ethics of intersubjectivity would be difficult to imagine.

The solipsistic eroticism of the *hermana*'s project is characteristic of a lack of intersubjective reciprocity on the part of all the furies. Like her, each radically fails to consider others as anything but objects and is unwilling to appeal to collaboration on any we-project. There is no diegetic other to meet the *hermana*'s imploring gaze (only a likely unwilling viewer); on the street no contact is made; and her seduction of the boyfriend, whose drunken desperation for sexual release amounts to lack of consent on his part, is, in its solipsism, worthy of Sade. While Beauvoir calls for the abandonment of oneself in the sexual experience to the emotional intoxication and vulnerability that allows for the formation of a bond with the other, sex for the furies is radically lonely, lacking any intersubjective appeal to create a community that might move beyond immanence. This lack of reciprocity reiterates and solidifies the facticity of the situation of both self and other.

Later, viewer expectations are further shattered when the *hija*, instead of being crushed by the news that her fiancé slept with her aunt, laughs it off in an unsentimentalized, antimelodramatic reaction, possibly understanding it as an indicator of his sexual desperation. She is less interested in romantic love than in using sex to achieve what she most desires, freedom from the stifling home, in yet another project that fails to encourage the other's freedom and instead strives for his submission. It is surely no coincidence that this critique of morality in which the apparently virtuous daughter suffers misfortune, only to respond with laughter, appears in the first Argentine film directed by a woman in forty years.

Lah's use of Elsa Daniel in this role is further charged by its departure from the actress's previous well-known appearances in films directed by Leopoldo Torre Nilsson, the internationally successful pioneering auteur of Argentine cinematic modernism. Daniel was the fetish actress of the director, appearing in three of his films prior to 1960, including *La casa del ángel* (1957), in which she played naive teenagers undergoing sexual awakenings.[14] In these films, adapted from novels by Beatriz Guido, her characters are "heroines with ambivalent feelings toward the house they live in, fearful or intimidated by their surroundings or actively penetrating into prohibited spaces as a transgressive preview of an identity and a sexuality both alien to the law of the father" (Amado 356). While in the Torre Nilsson/Guido films Daniel's character desires, yet is fearful due to her innocence, her character in *Las furias* has moved from timid youthful ambivalence into unsentimental cynicism and an utterly utilitarian conception of love and sex. Her choices have already fully defined her character, and she has taken charge (albeit in bad faith) of her sexuality in a way that the heroines of the Torre Nilsson/Guido films are incapable of doing. Where her characters there had "a physical attitude between rigid and languid, automatic and ghostly, with a childish, reedy voice on the edge of audibility, stammering, inarticulate" (360), the virginity of Daniel's character in *Las furias* is due instead to her lucidly cynical awareness of the power of her sexuality. She retains her virginity confidently, as a valuable object of exchange with which she might submit a male other to her will. Daniel herself noted the novelty of Lah's casting choice when asked to describe her character in an interview: "She's a self-centered and cynical girl, very calculating. She loves no one but herself and she wants to get out of that horrible house that overwhelms her. I'm very happy to play her, since it's a very different role from those I've played until now" ("Se reúnen las furias" 4). Such a casting against type of Daniel mires her character, along with the other furies, in the facticity of domestic and social institutions and an engagement with the world mediated by industrial culture made for women, an external source of values that presents illusory consumerist options that serve the immediate and already determined purposes of consumer capitalism and encourage them to flee from their own freedom into bad faith.

By contrast, the *amante* engages with the world actively yet with reciprocity, cultivating the freedom of Marcelo in a we-project that he embraces as well. Her actions, then, potentially transcend the limits of the present, going beyond themselves in space and time and in turn encouraging the freedom of others. The economic power she gains in business allows her both to overcome subordination to man and to disrupt the existing oppressive order of the domestic space, thus introducing to Argentine filmic culture a myth "outside the beautiful tyranny of the feminine" (Castillo 49), a woman who transcends the civilized condition described in

Beauvoir's famous dictum and the explanation that followed it: "One is not born, but rather becomes, a woman. No biological, psychic, or economic destiny defines the figure that the human female takes on in society; it is civilization as a whole that elaborates this intermediary product between the male and the eunuch that is called feminine" (*The Second Sex* 283). In no way like a eunuch, the *amante* escapes the trap that imposes the feminine condition so deplored by Beauvoir, becoming perhaps the first in the national cinema to answer her call to a relationship of generous equality: "Living together is an enrichment for two free beings, who find a guarantee of their own independence in the partner's occupations; the self-sufficient wife frees her husband from the conjugal slavery that was the price of her own. If the man is scrupulously well-intentioned, lovers and spouses can attain perfect equality in undemanding generosity" (*The Second Sex* 733). Due to her actions in the business world, the *amante* is able to assume economic responsibility for her and Marcelo's freedom, in a reciprocal relationship that contrasts starkly with the hierarchical, thus confining, relationship of Marcelo with the furies, who live in bad faith, failing to recognize or embrace their own freedom. This notion of freedom extends to the realm of marriage, both in Beauvoir and in *Las furias*, where it is anchored to the specific institutional facticity of Argentine divorce law.

Beauvoir's ideas on marriage also prove useful to an understanding of the film's climax. She holds that the decision to form part of a couple should be an active and constantly made choice, instead of a bad-faith flight into the security of a static institution. In *Las furias*, the *amante*, divorced, working and creating on the same plane as men, becomes their economic equal and thus embodies Beauvoir's modern woman who, through projects of her own creation, transcends the repetitiveness and lack of creativity that characterize the immanence of woman's condition. The *amante*'s relationship with Marcelo takes the form of a project undertaken as a couple, and can therefore potentially transcend the limits of their facticity. But as for Beauvoir freedom is not radical, but rather "situated, subject not only to the whims of embodiment but also to those of historical, social location" (Andrew 33), so it is in the film. The furies' freedom not only is limited by their own bad faith but also is compounded by the social institution of marriage and the lack of accessible divorce. Although the *madre* and the *hija* (due to the financial advantage implied by an alliance with the wealthy *amante*) want the *esposa* to agree to a separation, the law requires mutual consent, which she refuses to grant. As Beauvoir had written in *The Second Sex*, "The woman confined to immanence tries to keep man in this prison as well; thus the prison will merge with the world, and she will no longer suffer from being shut up in it" (754). The lack of legal divorce—as the *madre* says, "frente a las leyes de nuestro país, tú serás siempre su esposa legítima" (according to the laws of our country, you will always be the legitimate wife)—allows the *esposa* to block the reciprocal project of Marcelo and the *amante*, saying, "Ahora somos cuatro contra uno, contra el hombre. ¿No vamos a poder con él las cuatro?" (Now we're four against one, against the man. The four of us will be stronger than him, right?). An arranged separation would both ease the financial straits of the household and allow Marcelo and the *amante* to transcend its facticity, yet the insistence by the *esposa* on preserving her position thwarts such a resolution, at least for a time.

The *amante*'s money eventually proves too tempting for the furies, and as the *hija* says, the restrictive divorce law "es para los tontos, con dinero se resuelve todo" (is for idiots, with money anything can be fixed). After arguments and negotiations, the furies have finally reached an agreement in which the *esposa* is willing to concede a separation in exchange for the *amante*'s payment of "una suma elevada de dinero" (a large sum of money), but then the *amante* suddenly appears at the door and enters the room where the furies are seated around a table. As the camera tracks toward her, she announces dramatically that Marcelo has died at his office of a heart attack.

In the denouement, the *amante*, now lacking a we-project, appears to forsake her independent status and join the furies. Since one cannot choose her situation, her freedom is limited to choosing within it. The stubborn resistance of the factic may have put an end to the *amante*'s freedom, but in her short-lived gesture toward transcendence, Lah reflects the ethical dimension of Beauvoir's early work. Beauvoir's ethics formulate an imperative to embrace freedom, and the failure to do so is bad-faith complicity. The furies, trapped in the home, refuse to recognize the others' freedom, and as such fail to realize their own. Although one woman takes up the call to liberation and to ethical engagement with the world, facticity dooms her to a failure that, by the end of the film, defeated, she recognizes, entering the bad-faith community of the furies. But the space of this community is soon destroyed, literally, when at the film's end the house is seen under demolition to make way for the construction of an apartment tower. Grim implications of such urban development are many, but this could also be seen symbolically as an inevitable liberation, since the space of domestic oppression has ceased to exist, replaced by a future in which the furies are cast out unprepared into society and a freedom not taken on their own terms.

But earlier the film articulates a space of conditional freedom for women in this future, in the sequence added by Lah in her adaptation of Suárez de Deza's play, which takes place in the *amante*'s office. Lah here introduces to the national cinema a new myth of woman: a space created by the *amante* through her own actions as an entrepreneur, in which a woman achieves economic independence. The creation of this space allows the character to transcend domestic immanence and forge a relationship of reciprocity with the film's lone male character, a transcendence that, however short-lived, for the spectator remains a challenge in the form of a public space into which women venture to liberate themselves, one that would have to wait twenty years to be represented again in Argentine cinema, by Bemberg.

It is easy to understand why *Las furias* did not achieve success with the public or critics at the time of its release, since it conveys an untimely glimpse of women's condition—a Beauvoir-resonant film a full decade before the wide embrace of second-wave feminism in Argentina—and radically, if only fleetingly, confronts the conventionally gendered mechanics of the cinematic gaze. The end of the film, though, neutralizes any possible optimism and makes clear a need for more robust feminist responses. That the contemporary reviews of the film failed to understand its Beauvoirian affinities is made evident by descriptions of the totality of the female characters, including the *amante*, as furies. One reviewer of the time wrote of all the female characters, including the *amante*: "In all, one or another form of egoism. In all, the desire to break him in some way. In all, finally, the moral blame for his death" ("Escasa fortuna de un Debut" n. pag.). Like this reviewer, the important trade journal for film exhibitors, *Heraldo del Cinematografista*, also failed to clearly distinguish between the *amante* and the other female characters: "Due to its theme, it is a special entertainment for a feminine audience, since it exploits problems of interest to women: the mother whose excessive and obsessive love for her son leads her to provoke the unhappiness of all; the wife who has lost the affections of her mother and daughter; the spinster sister, eternally neglected, who one day tragicomically rebels against her situation; the other woman, who cannot consummate in matrimony her love for a married man; and the daughter, empty of affection, who only thinks of a marriage of convenience to escape the family she disdains" ("Las furias" 314). This anonymous critic reads *Las furias* in the terms of the "women's film," which, to put it bluntly, tends to offer lessons to a female viewership on how to preserve patriarchy. Such a misreading points toward a reason for the film's lack of attention from the local public and critics. *Las furias* appears to have been ahead of its time in its critical understanding of gender and ethics, screening a full decade before the arrival to Argentina of a second-wave feminism that also took much of its inspiration from Beauvoir.

Lah's second and final film was screened in 1963. She cowrote the script of *Las modelos* with Abelardo Arias, the well-known novelist more recently recognized for his editorial work and queer networking. Recent archival discoveries have begun to reveal Arias's secretive but committed activism in the transatlantic queer cultural networks that connected the French organization Arcadie and the Argentine gay community (Guzzante). In addition to the film's engagement with women's situation, it includes a representation of a gay man that makes clear the psychological devastation of the closet, a kind of representation that would not be seen again until the 1970s.

But the primary focus of *Las modelos* is an issue present in *The Second Sex*, that of the stubborn facticity at the intersection of class and gender that results in women's economic dependence on men. The film, firmly set in Argentine social-class reality, reflects Beauvoir's ideas perhaps even more rigorously than does *Las furias*, in its exploration of the very limited domain of possibilities within which many working-class women must make life-defining decisions, especially regarding their relationships with men. The film assumes, that is, that in the situation of most women in the Argentina of its time, economic facticity limits freedom to the point that it is not possible to renounce the protection of a man. Here Lah anticipates Bemberg's feature films, both those she scripted and those she directed, which narrate the often unsuccessful struggles of female protagonists to achieve a degree of independence, although in *Las modelos* the protagonists are of more modest means than Bemberg's elites and thus are forced to make decisions within an even more circumscribed domain of possibilities. *Las modelos* sets out to explore the consequences and ethical implications of the scant options available within the situation of economically disadvantaged young women. Although due to its pessimistic existentialism it might today appear challenging to argue for the inclusion of the film in a feminist tradition, in the context of the Argentine cinema of its time, *Las modelos* is an utterly unique exploration of the intersection of economics and gender through women's perspectives.

The workplace options for women are very limited in the film, and the two protagonists, Ana and Sonia (played by Mercedes Alberti and Greta Ibsen), are not wealthy. They work long hours as models in a designer's showroom, showing off clothes to wealthy, mostly female clients, while earning little pay. Lah does not shy away from the factic frame within which the best opportunity these women have to better their situation is to take advantage of their physical attributes and manage their relationships with wealthier men so that they might articulate a somewhat reciprocal project and transcend their economic conditions. By the film's end, Ana will have managed a modest transcendence of her situation by bringing her lover into a relationship of relative reciprocity and a common project that goes beyond the mere temporary benefit of selling her beauty, while Sonia will have fled her freedom into the bad faith of just such a purely instrumental relationship. The viewer witnesses the decisions that lead each to this conclusion within the scant freedom possible in their situation.

This examination of gendered practices from the perspectives of female protagonists subjects masculinity to a thoroughly critical vision. The gendered practices put under examination are those of Argentina, and more specifically of Buenos Aires, and the gaze of the *mendocina* Ana is, like those of Lah and Arias, that of an outsider. The opening credits are seen over a montage of publicity images featuring female models, which activates a key factor in the film's exploration of women's situation, that of the commodification of feminine beauty. The film then focuses on its two protagonists. Sonia begins the film involved in what to her seems a happy romance with a much wealthier man (played by a young Jorge Hilton), while Ana has trouble finding love, in part due to her being more distrustful of men's intentions and insistent on certain conditions in a relationship. As the film proceeds, their trajectories will take opposite directions as a result of their choices. For Sonia these result in a lack of a reciprocal project, since, when her wealthy boyfriend leaves her to marry a woman of his own social class, she rebounds into the arms of an older, wealthy, untrustworthy, and unattractive businessman whose relationship with her takes the form of a quid pro quo in which economic security is exchanged for beauty and sex, with clearly very little reciprocity. Ana's insistence that her relationship not be such a conventionally economic exchange allows her to eventually determine its relatively reciprocal conditions.

As the film begins, Sonia is unworried about her relationship with Carlos, her wealthy boyfriend, while Ana is distrustful of men's motives. She appears calculating, opining that a woman must be cunning and levy her physical attractiveness to manage relationships on her own terms. Sonia stakes out her own more disinterested yet ingenuous position, saying that "jamás aceptaría nada de Carlos . . . nos gozamos en la misma proporción, el amor es recíproco. . . . Yo creo en la igualdad de los sexos" (I would never accept anything from Carlos . . . we enjoy ourselves in the same proportion, our love is reciprocal. . . . I believe in the equality of the sexes). Ana's reply demonstrates a more lucid consciousness of their situation:

> La igualdad de los sexos, según tu interpretación, está bien para las ricas. . . . En nuestro caso [as nonwealthy women] el amor debe también rendir. Y ellos lo comprenden. Y si tiene clase, sabe disimularlo con regalos, etcétera, etcétera. . . . Como modelos nunca saldremos de pobres.
>
> Equality of the sexes, according to your interpretation, is fine for rich women. . . . In our case [as nonwealthy women] love should also pay. And they know that. And if he has class, he'll know how to dissimulate with gifts, et cetera, et cetera. . . . As models we'll always be poor.

Sonia's optimism might be more idealist and appealing, but it is based on inexperience, while Ana's position, which sounds exceedingly cynical and even immoral—and which under the classical cinema's conventions would call for her punishment as moral compensation—will later be revealed to better reflect a Beauvoirian situated ethics.[15]

Ana has two suitors, the economically powerful *estanciero* (rancher) Jorge and the relatively modest architect Luis, and the competition between them presents choices to her that explore a situated ethics of reciprocity. When Sonia asks her which man she prefers, Ana replies with lucidity: "No me hago ilusiones. Sé lo que quieren de mí. ¿O te crees que por ir a una estancia ya somos chicas de la buena sociedad? En la buena sociedad están solamente los hombres" (I have no illusions. I know what they want from me.

Or do you think that by going to an *estancia* we're now high-society women? In high society there are only men). But Ana soon perceives differences in the attitude of each suitor. After the wealthy Jorge invites the two friends to a party at his *estancia*, where he surprises the invitees by having them witness a bull having sex with a cow as part of the artificial insemination process, Ana confirms her disgust at Jorge's will to shock in a subsequent conversation with her other suitor, Luis, who states that "Jorge fue siempre el mismo, le gusta escandalizar por pura pose, jugar al toro por interpósita persona" (Jorge was always the same, he likes to scandalize as a pose, to play at being a bull through an intermediary). Ana's response makes her attitude clear: "¿Me perdonará si le digo que es un mal generalizado entre los latinoamericanos? . . . Ustedes tienen la obsesión de la masculinidad" (Will you forgive me if I say that that's a common condition among Latin American men? . . . You have an obsession with masculinity). That a female character speaks the word "masculinity" is in itself notable in a film made in 1963 and indicates a novel configuration in the cinema, one in which a woman's perspective on men is explored, but Lah will depart even further from convention with this film.

Despite being less wealthy than Jorge, Luis soon begins to win the competition for Ana, and the inverse progression of the parallel story lines of the two models' relationships articulates an ever-clearer contrast. Sonia's boyfriend, Carlos, gets engaged to a woman of his own social class and suggests to Sonia that she continue seeing him as his mistress, while Ana and Luis start a relationship, albeit in fits and starts. Luis tries clichéd methods of seduction, which Ana rejects; then he tries to tempt her with his wealth. But Ana asserts herself in an attempt to forge a relationship that might be based as much on her terms as on his: "No quiero que me traten como una aventura más" (I don't want to be treated as just another adventure).

Where Sonia, in bad faith, after her breakup with Carlos decides to settle for the security offered by a relationship with an unattractive and vulgar, yet wealthy businessman, Ana clearly recognizes the danger of such purely economic arrangements that embrace the commodification of woman. In the preliminaries of her relationship with Luis, she strives to achieve recognition of her subjectivity and a degree of reciprocity, although the degree to which this is possible is limited by the facticity of her situation. Luis gives Ana a much-desired penthouse apartment and appears to acknowledge that any relationship with her can only be reciprocal. That this may seem like a modest achievement on Ana's part appears to be the point of the film, which in its pessimism echoes Beauvoir's comparison of men's and women's situations: "If these same situations are compared, it is obvious that the man's is infinitely preferable, that is to say, he has far more concrete opportunities to project his freedom in the world" (*The Second Sex* 664). This thought reminds us that the limitations imposed by the factic allow for a very limited field of effective freedom for women, which helps explain the smile on the face of Ana as the film ends. For her, the possibility of even limited transcendence of her situation within a relationship of reciprocity brings euphoria when compared with expectations of a dreary, repetitive future of selling her beauty to the highest bidder. Her actions are contrasted with Sonia's failure to embrace her freedom, which for Beauvoir is bad faith, the trap set by a patriarchal society in which it is more immediately comfortable for women to reject their freedom than to take responsibility for it. This distinction between bad faith and a difficult freedom is at stake in the actions of the two protagonists of *Las modelos*, as well as those of the *hija* and the *amante* in *Las furias*, with which Lah's limited filmography formulates a powerful critique of Argentine cinema's conventional treatment of an unexamined traditional marriage as the nonnegotiable destiny of its female characters.

It could be argued that the modesty of the film's hope for women, its apparent pessimism, reflects the socially embedded subjectivity of women in Argentina of its time, and there resides the power of its denunciation, which echoes Beauvoir: "Yes, women in general *are* today inferior to men; that is, their situation provides them with fewer possibilities: the question is whether this state of affairs must be perpetuated" (*The Second Sex* 12–13; emphasis in original). A consciousness of such a situation is the first step toward its transcendence, as the precondition of the kind of common project of generosity and collective freedom that might go beyond the sphere of the couple and appeal to others to accompany it into the future, an emancipatory project that in the context of Argentina would be more widely embraced only in the 1970s, by Bemberg and others.

In *Las modelos*, another existential situation explored, though in a less comprehensive way, is that of a gay man in a strongly homonegative culture. The film's portrayal of a gay character as psychologically complex antedates those referred to by Guillermo Olivera when he writes that "despite the authoritarian political context that dominated the country during most of the 1960s and 1970s, the so-called 'socio-analytic tradition' . . . of Argentine cinema made possible the perhaps-first complex, non-unidimensional representations of LBGTQ persons in the Argentine cinema" (103). Olivera goes on to mention specifically one film from 1961 and three from the mid-1970s. *Las modelos* is, unsurprisingly, since it is so little known, not on his list.

Although the film's character of Pierre, an haute couture designer, is somewhat stereotypical when in his showroom, it is made clear that while away from work he is closeted. His need for the closet and a *pantalla*—a word best translated into English as "beard"—raises the issue of the lack of social acceptance and the resulting psychological trauma. This depiction is unique in the Argentine cinema of the time, which, as Olivera describes, had to take great care not to indicate explicitly that any character was gay: "The Argentine films of the sixties and seventies undertook a certain *indirect inclusion*—although no longer 'exclusionary' or discriminatory as they were in the previous period—of nonheteronormative characters and performativities, which today could be read as *queer*, but which in those stories could not be designated . . . as homosexual or trans identities" (103). In contrast to the representations described by Olivera, Pierre's identity as a gay man—along with the resulting social marginalization, delegitimization, and psychological devastation—is made clear in a sequence in which he asks

Sonia to marry him. A distraught Sonia, whose wealthy boyfriend has just left her in order to marry a woman of his own social class, angrily responds: "¡Querés casarte conmigo para que te sirva de pantalla y te crean un hombre normal! ¡Cualquier día!" (You want to marry me so I'll be your beard and people will think you're a normal man! Right, any day now!). Pierre, clearly anguished by her response, lashes out verbally not only at Sonia but also at the others working in the showroom. As a gay man inhabiting a heteronormative order (outside of his workplace, that is) and struggling with the psychological toll implied by such an existence, Pierre's situation is one of radical limitations.

Lah's film, then, can be considered an early example of what Olivera calls "queer performativities that open spaces of queer social visibility, although on the condition that it is a marginal and marginalizing spatialization" (104; emphasis in original). *Las modelos*' example of a queer visibility antedates those films discussed in depth by Olivera—*La Raulito* (Lautaro Murúa, 1974) and *La tregua* (Sergio Renán, 1974)—by a decade, a fact less important as trivia than as a point of entry into a discussion of the film's exploration of facticity, its articulation of a kind of queer existentialism. Olivera describes the 1970s cinema as the period of "inclusion of gay or trans characters who inhabit . . . socially marginal spaces, in a movement of drift within a diegetic world that Julianne Pidduk . . . has called an 'underground pre-visibility world.' . . . These films, by not following an affirmative agenda of new LGBT identities, did not open a new identitary rhetorical space, but they did inaugurate a certain space of critical queer visibility . . . capable of problematizing the heteronormative order of the social spaces that their characters inhabit through a critique that operated between subversion and symptom" (105).

Olivera here identifies a key point for understanding Lah's films as critical interventions not only in terms of the gay character Pierre, but also for their female characters: the lack of an affirmative agenda, indeed its impossibility, is imposed by the specific facticity of the Argentina of the early 1960s, in which Lah and Arias situate not only the two female characters but also Pierre. Not at all optimistic fantasies of liberation, Lah's films contain female and gay male characters firmly situated in their realities, a choice that allows the films to rigorously explore the limitations that the factic imposes on their freedom to enact projects. These are by force not affirmative representations and thus may, for many of today's spectators, prove unrecognizable as feminist, queer-positive, or otherwise liberatory. But despite this impossibility of affirmative representations, in the case of Pierre this is not a strategy of "exclusionary inclusion" (105) that characterized the homophobic representations of the period of 1930–1960, the "previous regime of representation that tended to reduce homosexualities to caricatures, negative stereotypes (criminal and/or pathological) or to the inclusion of homosexual characters as a mere source of humor through derision or mocking, in the service of a heteronormative plot" (106). Unlike such representations, those of Lah's films renounce both negative stereotyping and optimistic celebration, to instead explore the embodied existence of women and gay men whose freedom is starkly limited by facticity. To do so is to call to consciousness the factic, and thus take a step toward the creation of the conditions in which it might be possible to imagine and act toward a future in which this same factic situation might be transcended. As Barbara S. Andrew writes, "Women are so situated in patriarchal society that choosing against themselves may seem to be the only way to choose. But, once one becomes aware of the possibility of liberation, one must act. Otherwise one is in bad faith" (28). Although Lah's films depict situations in which action is possible and the line between authenticity and bad faith is clear, they are not optimistic and as such are grim viewing experiences and difficult to identify as liberatory works of art.

According to an anonymous reviewer of the film in the daily *La Nación* on October 19, 1963, *Las modelos* tells "an elemental story, loaded with ingenuousness and conventionalisms. It develops on a capriciously anecdotal level, behind which it is useless to look for anything that has meaning or transcendence, even though at times a vague allusion to society is included" ("Un film con forma y fondo" n. pag.). While this reviewer was blind to *Las modelos'* exploration of women's situation, seeing in it nothing more than a capricious collection of anecdotes, if we turn again to Beauvoir, the film's value becomes clear: "Literature is born when something in life goes slightly adrift . . . the first essential condition is that *reality should no longer be taken for granted*; only then can one both perceive it, and make others do so" (qtd. in Andrew 42). It could be said that Lah's films, in their emphasis on the facticity specific to midcentury Argentina and, thus, their refusal to take reality for granted, had recognized something adrift about life in Argentina. But judging by their brief theatrical runs and by reviews written at the time, this refusal had little resonance with the public and critics.[16]

María Herminia Avellaneda directed *Juguemos en el mundo* (1971), though the film is as much a creation of María Elena Walsh, who had invented its characters years before for a play of the same name, wrote its script, and acted and sang in the film. Together they created a self-funded production company, Producciones Tami, and shot the film on location in the town of Pasteur, in Buenos Aires Province, where Avellaneda had spent her early years.

As the political situation in Argentina became more conflictive during the 1970s, Walsh, already widely loved as a poet, writer, and singer of whimsical works for both child and adult audiences, responded creatively, as K. M. Sibbald describes: "With changes in the socio-political climate in Argentina . . . the light-heartedness of much of the early whimsy faded as, in 1977, in *Chaucha y Palito*, Walsh felt constrained to argue more directly in favor of social justice and greater tolerance of difference" (1997, 851). A consideration of the filmic version of *Juguemos en el mundo* shifts the date of this politicization much earlier in the decade, to the long-running period of military governments begun with that of Onganía in 1966.

Walsh's consciousness of gender-based injustices dates to much further in the past. She was a longtime reader of feminist authors and, as in the case of many other women actively producing in the

Argentine cultural field, recognizes her inspiration in Beauvoir's *The Second Sex*. Luraschi and Sibbald write that

> María Elena Walsh's feminist praxis originates in her insistent way of considering *The Second Sex* . . . as a "catechism" or "the Bible" of the movement. More than forty years after the appearance of one of the key works of feminist thought, the insistence by the Argentine writer is surprising, since, though all recognize Beauvoir as the great theorist of the movement, few cite the early arguments she laid out in that book. . . . A voracious reader, Walsh knows and recognizes the diverse contributions of Betty Friedan, Kate Millett, Susan Gubar and Sandra Gilbert, Hélène Cixous, Luce Irigaray and Julia Kristeva, among others, but she does not cite them as influences. The contrary occurs, nevertheless, with Beauvoir: Walsh notes that that first reading in Paris, at the beginning of the fifties, is the start of her own awakening. (148)

The writers go on to quote Walsh directly on her revelatory experience of reading Beauvoir: "Then one reads *The Second Sex*, for example, and upon seeing in print what one has lived and carries engraved on her *criollo* heart, one wakes up" (148). Walsh leaves little doubt as to her intellectual and affective lineage, and in *Juguemos en el mundo* the filmmakers represent just such a feminist awakening of a young character, to which I will return.

The film's origins can be found in Walsh's songwriting and singing career, which she began upon forming a duo with Leda Valladares in Paris before turning to solo performances. Sibbald writes that with her solo career Walsh "virtually metamorphosized the urban folksong. For ten years from 1968 she enthralled audiences with her quizzical look at Argentine society, shot through with nostalgia, tenderness, solidarity, and, increasingly, anger at the persistent infringement of civil liberties in that period" (1997, 852). The play *Juguemos en el mundo* was first presented in 1968, in Buenos Aires's Teatro Regina, a collection of the lyrics of songs she performed during this time was published under the same title in 1970, and the film was released in August 1971.

Walsh brought many of the ideas, but the translation into audiovisual form was the work of Avellaneda, with whom she had enjoyed a long romantic relationship marked by frequent artistic collaboration, as Sibbald recounts: "Walsh had become acquainted with María Herminia Avellaneda in 1958, when she was still living with Leda Valladares; by 1966 she had moved in with Avellaneda and shared with her new ventures of writing television soaps, organizing her show for children *Canciones para mirar* (1962), planning the film *Juguemos en el mundo* (1971), scheduling *Cuentopos* for Spanish television, and arranging Walsh's *début* at the Teatro Maipo in a mix of *café-concert* and *music hall* that lasted until *Chau ejecutivo* in 1978" (2010, 219–220). Avellaneda is known primarily as a director of television, where she began as an assistant director in 1955, and theater, on which she collaborated extensively with Walsh, directing in 1963 her *Doña Disparate y Bambuco*, a "somewhat clownesque musical comedy that relies on nonsensicality and eventually becomes a stairway to the infinite, where each stair creates absurdities from the sound and rhythm of the words, with the exaggerated and opportune movement of the true clowns, inheritors of the commedia dell'arte" (Boland 72–73). The titular characters of the play later appeared in *Juguemos en el mundo*, though the film's formulation of a complex critique of authoritarianism shifts its intended audience toward adults. First screened on August 19, 1971, the film opens as a romantic, antimodern, and individualist rebellion against bourgeois, suit-clad urban conformity, in which the two protagonists, instead of traveling from Buenos Aires to Paris as they did in the play, move from the capital to the countryside, before revealing the naïveté of the nonconformists' romantic rebellion when faced with sinister authority figures and compliant citizens.

Doña Anémona Disparate (played by Perla Santalla) and Bambuco (Jorge Mayor) only know the nation's rural spaces through the optic of a national culture that had conventionally recurred to conservative *criollismo*'s images of rural space as an idyllic repository of a gaucho-centric national essence.[17] But despite its playful, nonrealist tone, the film links these antimodern *criollista* representations of rural space to authoritarian politics by representing the small town as dominated by a retrograde patriarchy, where life is anything but idyllic, especially for women. There is no character who might act as an authorized voice of reason (except possibly Walsh herself, in an extended appearance near the end of the film), since the two protagonists themselves are immersed in the national culture's conventional conception of rural space. As they set off from Buenos Aires for the countryside in an antique jalopy and under the thrall of romantic optimism, Doña Disparate informs a passerby, "Nos vamos a vivir al campo, hartos de la vida ciudadana. Sí, nos vamos a vivir al campo, a algún pueblecito gauchesco" (We're off to live in the country, sick of city life. Yes, we're off to the live in the country, to some gauchesque little town). The perspectives of these two protagonists are here ironized as ingenuous products of a national culture that has long tended to nostalgically represent the nation's rural spaces as a repository of a premodern authenticity. Doña Disparate's dreamy optimism and bourgeois class sympathies leave her in denial of the reality of her surroundings, while the naive but industrious Bambuco is only slightly more down-to-earth.

Upon arrival, instead of a pastoral refuge from the stresses of the modern city, they encounter a town under the steely will of a mysterious character posting absurd rules and regulations: "Prohibido sembrar flores hoy" (Planting flowers prohibited today) and "Prohibido estacionar de 0 a 24 horas" (Parking prohibited between 0 and 24 hours). This authoritarian figure, the descriptively named Doctor Heriberto Mandoni (played by Norman Briski), is accompanied by a troop of identically top-hatted and black-clad men wearing masks, short pants, and striped knee socks. These comic-serious enforcers are called "Prepos" (short for *prepotentes*, a term used to describe arrogant abusers of power). Mandoni is an obviously allegorical figure, though it is difficult to unambiguously identify a referent, since he is a comically distilled embodiment of many possible historical and contemporary representatives of repressive power. Despite (or because of) his heavy hand, no public services function: the post office, the telephones, the trains, none operate, and the local newspaper is *clausurado* (closed by official order). Such a representation of authority as overbearing and incompetent is unsurprising in its context, after ten years of Perón (whom Walsh vehemently opposed) followed by intermittent periods of military dictatorship, most recently the long-running sequence of Onganía, Levingston, and Lanusse, which was rapidly losing control of the nation and would soon allow Peronism's participation in politics and the eventual return of the exiled leader to the presidency.

The links between social class and support for (anti-Peronist) authoritarianism are revealed when the protagonists, out searching for fuel, encounter a couple living in a shack that functions as a metonymy for the spatial and economic marginality of the *villa miseria*. The dysfunctionality of public services has stunted progress, immiserating the poor even further, and a woman inhabitant responds that no fuel is available—"Y . . . hace mucho que está faltando la nafta" (There hasn't been any gasoline for a long time now)—before explaining that neither buses nor telephones work either. By contrast, Doña Disparate's response betrays her more bourgeois class sympathies: "¡Esto no puede ser, Bambuco, ni trenes, ni correos, ni conciertos sinfónicos, ni nada!" (This can't be, Bambuco, no trains, nor postal service, nor symphony concerts, nothing!). When she is distracted from the poverty and authoritarian abuses by the arrival of what she excitedly refers to as the "beautiful people, la gente distinguida de la localidad" (the beautiful people, the distinguished persons of the locality), her hopes rise.

The local bourgeoisie is favored by Mandoni's policies and supports him wholeheartedly, reflecting the widespread self-serving complicity with the recurring military coups in the 1950s and 1960s. By contrast, the allegiances of the film itself are made clear when Mandoni pronounces a self-legitimizing discourse that could have been spoken by Onganía:

> La juventud de hoy necesita una guía, un oriente. . . . Nosotros tenemos que ser una antorcha en el camino de esa juventud descarriada que olvida el ideal de sus mayores . . . en la alcaldía controlamos muy bien la llegada de artistas y de todo lo que atente contra nuestro estilo de vida.
>
> The youth of today needs a guide, a point of orientation. . . . We must be a light on the road for that wayward youth that is forgetting the ideals of its elders . . . in City Hall we monitor very closely the arrival of artists and all of those who might threaten our lifestyle.

In office, Onganía zealously combated foreign influence, especially in youth culture and universities. Similarly, in *Juguemos en el mundo*, youth, artists, dreamers, and nonconformists in general are demonized as threats by Mandoni, who, in a prescient justification of repressive state violence, describes how they will be dealt with: "Ya acabaremos con los ciudadanos improductivos, todos los que no colaboran, mancomunados para hacer la grandeza de este rinconcito de esperanza nacional" (We'll soon finish off the unproductive citizens, all of those who don't collaborate, united to bring about the greatness of this little corner of national hope). Much like Onganía, Mandoni's discourse of progress and prosperity is, predictably, at odds with his actions, which cause the economy to stagnate and retard progress as he desperately holds on to a national ideal produced by restorative nostalgia. But in the film, state violence is more laughable than harsh, and resistance spreads even to the local schoolchildren, who block the main street by sitting across its dusty surface in a single-file picket line. The townsfolk eventually rise up in protest against Mandoni, who calls in the Prepos to repress the opposition. But, in keeping with the film's ludic tone, liberatory violence and state repression are allegorized as a tug-of-war between the Prepos and the popular opposition. At first it is an even match, but when the oversized local gaucho joins in, the pueblo emerges victorious. The victors angrily march to confront the never-seen alcalde (mayor), who, à la Wizard of Oz, proves to be a feeble old functionary of the Spanish Crown left over from the colonial period, powdered wig and all.

Bambuco, suddenly inspired into embarking on a do-it-yourself approach to solving the town's problems, fixes everything he can get his hands on: telegraph, phones, and so on. Eventually this industriousness leads the townsfolk to choose him and Doña Disparate to govern their newly liberated town. Among their first acts in office is the transformation of the post office into an "entidad autónoma destinada a mandar noticias agradables a quienes no suelen recibirlas" (autonomous entity dedicated to sending happy news to those who do not usually receive it) whose first chief is none other than María Elena Walsh, who arrives in town and sings several songs as all ends well.

Here the film dodges more serious political engagement to instead propose a notion of the power of culture to bring about solutions to society's worst problems, or to at least console the population with an illusion of individual freedom. Laraschi and Sibbald are generous in their evaluation of the film's politics, suggesting that "Walsh uses the film to suggest that with the classic feminine virtues (work, patience and nonviolence) it is possible to defeat abuse of power and bad government and bring about a reconstruction (typically feminine) in which education, public health and well-being are privileged" (179). This reading, while ignoring several aspects of the film—the central roles of Bambuco, the gaucho, and the pueblo in the liberation of the town—as well as the national reality of the burgeoning and increasingly violent opposition to the recent tradition of authoritarianism, does appreciate how the film's message of liberation also addresses women's condition across social classes. This is done in many ways, from the level of incidental dialogue to character exposition and the articulation of a major romantic plotline in exaggeratedly conventional gender terms.

In examples of the first two, in a sequence that takes place during a visit by Doña Disparate to a bourgeois home, when the man of the house orders the young servant, "¡A mí, chiquilina, cebáme unos mates!" (For me, girly, prepare me a *mate*!), she responds gamely with an insistence on recognition: "¡Me llamo Nancy!" (My name is Nancy!). In the same home, Doña Disparate is contracted to teach the remnant art of declamation to the daughter, Elvirita, who is first presented as a human doll, motionless in a huge plastic box. Doña Disparate's lesson elicits only tears and the anguished protest "¡Nunca tuve novio y me la paso mirando la tele como una tarada! ¡No quiero ser un ángel! ¡No quiero y no quiero!" (I've never had a boyfriend and I spend my time watching television like an idiot! I don't want to be an angel! I don't want to and I don't want to!). But when Doña Disparate consoles her by playing a lively tune on the piano, an inspired Elvirita tears off her tiara and dances wildly, suddenly liberated. While these exemplary secondary characters directly insist on recognition, a more thorough critique of women's situation under a specifically Argentine patriarchy is articulated around a romance involving Doña Disparate that exposes a repressive gender normativity deeply rooted in the national culture.

Doña Disparate is successfully courted by the gaucho Ramón Altamirano, who imagines a very traditional, in terms of gender, future with her:

> Soy viudo y ando necesitando alguna que cuide y limpie. . . . Tengo buen campo, una buena tropilla, casa de material pero en la cocina naides. Entonces, yo pensé, es pueblera, pero sana y trabajadora. No le va a hacer asco carnear un chancho o degollar una gallina.
>
> I'm a widower and need a woman to care for the house and clean. . . . I have a good plot of land, a good herd of cows, a solid house but no one in the kitchen. So, I thought, she's a city girl, but healthy and willing to work. She won't get disgusted butchering a hog or slaughtering a chicken.

Upon hearing this, Doña Disparate faints, having apparently fallen instantly in love with this oversized specimen of nationally ideal masculinity. From a modern feminist perspective informed by the notion of gender equality, Don Ramón is quite a sinister figure, as, at the same time, an embodiment of the national symbol of authenticity, a privileged object of romantic desire, and an unreflective enforcer of the traditional gender norms of patriarchy. This episode echoes what Walsh had written about her own past, that "in matters of courtship everything was very romantic as long as the girl obeyed" (2002, 127), combining whimsy with critique in a mode typical of the film.[18]

Laraschi and Sibbald claim that *Juguemos en el mundo* was not a success with the public, and they point toward possible problems with the film's politics: "The film disappeared from screens very quickly and sank into oblivion. In April of 1988 it was shown at the 'Woman in the Cinema' International Festival that took place in Mar del Plata. Although its author attributes the film's failure to the 'Cinema Machinery,' it is worth asking if its theme or intention were possibly deeper motives for that rejection" (46).[19] Despite these claims of failure, the box office reports in the *Heraldo del Cinematografista* show that the film was far from the flop described. Distributed by the powerful Aries Cinematográfica, it opened at number two in box office take in the capital, where it remained on screens for four weeks, a run comparable to that of the string of very popular films starring Palito Ortega at the time.

In the press, the film was reviewed widely and very positively. The well-respected critic Agustín Mahieu praised it as "imagination and poetry in a film of unprecedented audacity"; another, anonymous reviewer wrote that it was a "thorough demonstration that cinema made for a 'general public' need not be irrelevant or coarsely made" (qtd. in Manrupe and Portela 318).[20] Another press reviewer was enthusiastic enough about the film to call it "a captivating spectacle, enchanting, overflowing with vitality, freshness and fun" ("María Elena Walsh en un film lleno de humor" 12). Given these reviews and the partial box office reports, I find the evaluation of the film as a failure to be questionable, but regardless of whether it was a success or a failure, *Juguemos en el mundo* is doubtless one of the most politically cutting of commercial spectacles of its highly politicized moment.

In the years before she found worldwide success with her fiction feature films, María Luisa Bemberg made aesthetically radical shorts that are little known today. *El mundo de la mujer* (The world of women; 1972) and *Juguetes* (Toys; 1978) form part of the 1970s feminist militancy in Argentina of which Bemberg was a central figure as cofounder of the Unión Feminista Argentina. As an artist, Bemberg is unique in the context of Argentine feminism, since in it "the presence of visual artists was minor: although many were concerned with social change, they were not active in feminist movements nor did they develop a specifically feminist art in those years" (Andújar et al. 12). What most considered to be political art excluded feminist art, since, as Andrea Giunta writes, "feminism and party politics overlapped in a problematic way, and . . . in competition, to the point of attacks on the former by the latter. In those years accelerated by politics, the legitimacy of feminist interventions was questioned. These were considered part of a 'minor' politics that was delegitimized in function of the imperatives of another, 'major' politics" (2018, 81). Bemberg, in no way active in the early 1970s left or Peronist revolutionary political militancy, was one of the few cultural producers at the time to seek to legitimize the personal as a properly political concern and generator of artistic interventions.

She had begun a very active career in cultural production at a relatively late age. Born into one of Argentina's wealthiest families, she married within her class at age twenty-three. After a couple of decades of a traditionally domestic existence as wife and mother of four, she began to participate in theater during the 1960s, when she was in her forties, before moving into both film and feminist activism around 1970 (King 15). The latter activities came together when, after she wrote her first produced screenplay, *Crónica de una señora* (Raúl de la Torre, 1971), a feminist movement formed around Bemberg rather spontaneously. As Máximo Eseverri and Fernando Martín Peña describe, "in an interview about her script . . . Bemberg openly declared herself feminist and concerned with the relegation of women in all areas. As a consequence, she received numerous letters and phone calls from other women who wanted to organize themselves. Some of them then founded the Argentine Feminist Union (UFA) in the Café Tortoni, beneath the portrait of Alfonsina Storni" (170). While Bemberg's scriptwriting positioned her as a referent around whom others could gather, the swift reaction to her declaration indicates that there already existed a critical mass of women eager to exchange ideas and undertake collective action.

UFA nourished itself intellectually from texts written by European and North American feminists, a fact that would drive critiques of the movement as foreign to Argentina and, later, of Bemberg's feature films as ignoring the national reality lived by the widest sectors of the population. But this international inspiration could alternatively by seen as an example of what Adrienne Rich calls "resisting amnesia," or working against the trap in which "each new generation of feminists has been forced to document the most elementary exposition of the oppression of women yet again and also to repeat mistakes made by sisters of an earlier era" (1986, 147). The study by UFA's members of women's earlier responses to rapid consumerist modernization could be seen as a savvy appropriation of the lessons learned from those parallel experiences of their peers in the North. Its members were, in fact, quite diverse in both politics and class allegiance, and their readings were not restricted to any single feminism: "At a time when the space for women had expanded, many looked to the horizons for explanations of that which they needed to name. They started from their own previous experiences, from precise places and positions, each one covering different trajectories in her feminist becoming. That is why [Leonor] Calvera remembers [Shulamith] Firestone and the sisters of the north, while [Juliet] Mitchell is central for [Mirta] Henault, as is [Carla] Lonzi for [Gabriella] Christaller" (Rodríguez Agüero and Ciriza n. pag.). This list of foreign feminists demonstrates a wide scope of influence, but it lacks Bemberg's most frequently cited inspiration, Simone de Beauvoir, whose name, due to her foundational status, perhaps did not need to be mentioned.

Despite its diverse sources, UFA, like Argentine feminism in the 1970s more generally, was never widespread in terms of numbers.

Among the group's activities the most important was consciousness creation to produce new activists, as Giunta recounts: "UFA developed methods of consciousness creation, formulated from the Marxist/Leninist concept and practice of conscientization understood as a process of acquisition of class consciousness. Such practices were applied, in the case of second-wave feminism, to the acquisition of gender consciousness" (2014, 8). Bemberg's *El mundo de la mujer* formed part of this effort, which drew the attention of authorities after the return of Perón to the presidency in 1973 and the subsequent dominance of the movement by its violent right-wing sectors. With the presidency of Isabel Perón, the repression extended beyond that of the political left, and UFA was targeted by the Triple A, which raided the group's offices in 1974 (Giunta 2018, 100). This surveillance may seem surprising, yet it is understandable given the extreme gender traditionalism of the Peronist right in control at that time, as well as certain parallels between UFA's conscientization methods and those of the more well-known politically militant groups like the Montoneros and the Ejército Revolucionario del Pueblo, to which I will return.

UFA soon dissolved, and Bemberg went on to the more formally conventional feature-length narrative filmmaking for which she would become internationally known. The two short films she made in the 1970s have remained little studied, and the first was somewhat disavowed by Bemberg herself after her subsequent commercial success. Such a disavowal is understandable if seen from the perspective of her less radical, more formally conventional features, since the earlier work's avant-garde form articulates a far more confrontational feminism that shares with the revolutionary left militancy of the time certain provocations that might alienate sectors of a wider filmgoing public both in Argentina and internationally.[21] While care must be taken not to minimize the vast differences between the necessarily clandestine militancy in the interest of Marxism and/or revolutionary Peronism and the far less dangerous work of UFA, similarities can be seen not only in their form but also in their exhibition practices. Bemberg's shorts "were shown to groups of women in the interior of Argentina. First they watched the films, then began the sensitization talks. Mirta Henault recounts that she herself repeated this practice several times in the 1970s and early- 1980s. . . . The same happened with Lucrecia Oller, who tells of how Bemberg's shorts were often used to open the discussions, then the conversation would deepen with debates on the themes introduced by the shorts" (Trebisacce and Veiga 1410). The mobile distribution and exhibition of *El mundo de la mujer*, which consisted of semiclandestine showings to small audiences with time reserved for consciousness-raising discussions, replicates those of *La hora de los hornos*, in which the concept of the film-act leaves the film unfinished, to be completed by the actions of the audience on the social reality outside the theater. Andrea Giunta's description makes the influence explicit: "These conscientization groups were organized on the model of the cells of the armed organizations. Small groups of reflection and action composed of no more than eight activists and/or adherents, in which were discussed, based on readings and personal experiences, the causes of gender oppression" (2014, 8). It could be said, then, that these films were made under the assumption that the condition of women had changed to the point that Argentine society was ripe for a revolution, but it goes without saying that Bemberg's imagined revolution was not at all like that proposed by Cine Liberación. Unarmed and neither left, Peronist, nor a volatile combination of the two, this revolution was exclusively feminist, and the necessary conditions were present, in the opinion of many, for a widespread awakening to the connections between political and economic institutions and the resulting women's condition. As Shulamith Firestone, one of the northern inspirations of UFA with her 1970 book *The Dialectic of Sex: The Case for Feminist Revolution*, wrote: "Until a certain level of evolution had been reached and technology had achieved its present sophistication, to question fundamental biological conditions was insanity. Why should a woman give up her precious seat in the cattle car for a bloody struggle she could not hope to win? But, for the first time in some countries, the preconditions for feminist revolution exist—indeed, the situation is beginning to *demand* such a revolution" (3; emphasis in original).

Firestone posits that economic, social, and technological developments have finally made it possible to imagine a true feminist revolution, which brings with it an ethical obligation to act.[22] While stopping far short of Firestone's radical utopianism, in which, among other dreams, technology renders pregnancy superfluous, Bemberg's early short films also imply that the preconditions for true social change that might liberate women from their subordinate conditions were beginning to appear. She dares to imagine a reformulation of modern domesticity under which women's personal decision-making might no longer privilege the desires of a man.

Bemberg's intervention was part of a long-ongoing polemic in Argentine culture around the issue of femininity in the context of rapid modernization. Isabella Cosse examines this debate in the context of women's magazines in the mid-1960s, in which, she writes, a new, undomesticated model of femininity was finding wide circulation: "Against the grain of the imperatives taught until then, this prototype exalted the figures of young women who accepted sexual desire, with expectations of professional and work development and life plans that transcended matrimony and the home. In this way, between the late sixties and the early seventies, the transformation of the feminine model appeared to embark on a journey with no return: the prototype of the liberated young woman, already present a decade earlier, became radicalized, increasingly associated with the adjectives 'independent,' 'rebellious,' 'emancipated,' and defined the common sense of the new generation" (2009, 172–173). While the prototype described by Cosse was rapidly becoming more widespread, its growth did not go unanswered. An example of an important mass media presence in the debate was the women's magazine *Para Ti*. Cosse defines its place in the cultural field of the time:

> In 1965 *Para Ti* . . . was at the apogee of its renovation. In the following years it continued perfecting a new strategy to adapt to the changes of the time, which consisted of displaying an editorial line open to the transformations but with intentions to

influence the form these were taking. A rapid review of the titles of the articles of those years could give the impression that the magazine had taken the forefront in the struggle for women's liberation, as indicated in "protest" editorials on women's rights, women's work outside the home and the struggle against *machismo*. But that was not the case. It was, rather, a strategy based on accepting debate on the novelties with the objective of waging combat against them. (179)

The guise assumed by *Para Ti* of openness to new forms of femininity was later dropped as Argentine society became extremely polarized in the early 1970s and it became increasingly difficult to occupy a middle ground. Cosse writes that "with the political polarization already advanced in the seventies, *Para Ti* abandoned all receptivity to moderate progressivism, though it managed to maintain the illusion of impartiality. It would seem that, faced with the radicalization of the feminine model, the magazine stopped situating itself in an apparently middle ground, to instead mount an ideological attack in defense of the old domestic status quo" (180). So conspicuous was the gender traditionalism of the magazine at the time that Bemberg chose to quote it extensively in her first film, to which I will return.

In 1972, when Bemberg made *El mundo de la mujer*, Argentina was at the height of a wide-scale conflict that polarized society not only culturally but also politically. In such a context Bemberg's filmic intervention represents a radical statement against the traditionalist notions of femininity held by those in power (the long dictatorship that would soon come to an end), as well as by many of those who struggled against them. Although not at all in the interest of a left Peronist politics, the avant-garde form of *El mundo de la mujer* shares much with the revolutionary third cinema of Solanas and Getino's *La hora de los hornos*.[23] Bemberg's later profession of admiration for Solanas's filmmaking is revealing in its praise for its form but not its message: "He has an enviable freedom to manage situations and camera movements that are very interesting. I almost like more *how* he films than *what* he films"

(Trelles Plazaola 123). While *El mundo de la mujer* shares very little in the way of objectives with *La hora de los hornos*, the films do have a number of formal commonalities that locate both as modern inheritors of Soviet cinema. The use of associative montage of found images and sound to formulate an ironizing critique of the consumer culture spectacle and its publicity mechanisms is central to the two, and both climax with montage sequences of accelerating rhythm that produce a visceral appeal intended to prompt the spectator to action beyond the viewing experience. In the case of Bemberg's film, the desired reaction would be directed against the social construction of femininity that operated in synergy with the incipient consumerism that had intensified in Argentina during the 1960s. Catalina Trebisacce writes that *El mundo de la mujer* was critical of the "process that interpellated, seduced and affected particularly the population of women, the process of sociocultural modernization that had begun the previous decade. Modernization put these subjects into the center of the public, though not necessarily the political, scene. . . . The so-called 'modern woman' was on the cover of newspapers, magazines, and was the theme of debate on certain television programs that began to invade domestic afternoons. This stereotype of woman was also the object of interest and struggle of the feminists of the seventies, insofar as it was proclaimed the paradigm of women's liberation" (24). The commercial modernization described by Trebisacce, in which women's access to consumer goods increased without fundamentally altering their conditions in the gender order, is the clear target of the film's critique. To take Bemberg's own activism as exemplary, she envisions a woman who takes advantage of the opportunities brought by developmentalist modernization to transcend her situation, becoming a subject capable and worthy of liberation—a woman, that is, who enters the public scene on her own terms and as a political subject.

Instead of an aberration within her directorial career or a product of a militancy she would later renounce, *El mundo de la mujer* could be seen as Bemberg's first step toward the making of a "counter-cinema," to borrow a term Claire Johnston developed in an essay contemporary to the films. While not the type of film discussed by Johnston—the Hollywood features directed by Dorothy Arzner and Ida Lupino—these avant-garde shorts directly combat the practices by which women were represented not only in the cinema, in which "the image of man underwent rapid differentiation, while the primitive stereotyping of women remained with some modifications" (Johnston 22), but also those representations of women formulated by modern consumer culture more generally. The films display a clear awareness on the part of Bemberg of how the filmic image in itself is never innocent, tending to reflect what Johnston refers to as, in an expression very much of its time, "the dominant ideology," and how a filmmaker must actively intervene to instrumentalize the image if she is to combat media stereotyping of women:

> Clearly, if we accept that cinema involves the production of signs, the idea of non-intervention is pure mystification. The sign is always a product. What the camera in fact grasps is the "natural" world of the dominant ideology. Women's cinema cannot afford such idealism, the "truth" of our oppression cannot be "captured" on celluloid with the "innocence" of the camera: it has to be constructed/manufactured. New meanings have to be created by disrupting the fabric of the male bourgeois cinema within the text of the film. . . . Eisenstein's method is instructive here. In his use of fragmentation as a revolutionary strategy, a concept is generated by the clash of two specific images, so that it serves as an abstract concept in the filmic discourse. (29)

Much as Johnston prescribes, in her first film Bemberg intervenes through montage in order to disrupt the cultural construction of a privileged signifier in the ordering of female desire, that of bourgeois domesticity. The film's corresponding central motif of the palace is a myth imposed from childhood by such universal texts as *Cinderella*, one of the many stories that train young girls to aspire to the "happily-ever-after," yet nonreciprocal, telos of marrying into wealth. The motif of the sublime security of the palace is introduced early in the film, only to be reformulated by its end to suggest that quotidian domestic existence produces a very different condition, for which Bemberg will employ the metaphor of the prison.

El mundo de la mujer documents the commercial exposition Femimundo 72: La mujer y su mundo, held at the Buenos Aires fairgrounds of the Sociedad Rural Argentina, the association of the nation's traditional wealthy landowners. Unlike the films of Cine Liberación, which juxtaposed images of the Sociedad Rural with those of the social margins to denounce the realities that remained hidden in the national culture, this is a document of an already highly visible spectacle, and as such the imperative to instrumentalize the images and sounds is even more urgent. As we will see, Bemberg intervenes through montage to suggest that women exist in a relationship of colonized immanence in which their desires are subordinated to those of men, who occupy the role of the prince figure women have been trained to view as an object of aspiration.[24] María Laura Rosa succinctly describes Bemberg's strategy of denouncing the mediating role consumer culture plays in this relationship: "Bemberg's camera puts the emphasis on consumption as a ruse for eternal dependence on the man ... she exhibits the construction of an ideal of woman molded by patriarchy for the happiness of man. In her attentive and procreative role, woman finds herself trapped in a web that publicity and consumption contribute to legitimize and impose" (4). Since consumer culture hides its subjugating effects under the guise of freedom of choice, these effects are not immediately visible in its commodities, but by way of montage Bemberg disrupts this conventional specularity through which the expo mediates desires for its products.

If seen on its own, most of the film's footage could be considered a straightforward documentary, or even a celebration, of the spectacle mounted by Femimundo. But as Bemberg's intervention forces image to resonate against image, image against sound, and sound against sound, the resulting meanings undermine the discourse of a male voice-over that, reading from the expo catalog, reassures the female audience of its own privileged position in the modern regime of production and consumption, as an active subject whose desires the machinery of production functions to satisfy:

> Las firmas más importantes del país trabajan por . . . y para, usted. Por y para usted, su destinataria más importante. Las inquietudes, las curiosidades, las aspiraciones, los problemas, los sueños femeninos. Femimundo cambiará algo en su vida.
>
> Femimundo Sociedad Anónima organiza la primera muestra internacional de la mujer y su mundo. Todo lo nuevo que se produce en el país. Moda y elegancia, belleza, cosmética, alimentación, artículos del hogar. Femimundo Sociedad Anónoma, en base a profundos estudios y experiencias, realiza esta muestra, dirigiendo sus intereses y apelando por primera vez al más poderoso factor de consumo de la época actual: La mujer.

The most important companies in the country work because of . . . and for, you. Because of and for you, their most important addressee. Feminine worries, curiosities, aspirations, problems, dreams. Femimundo will change something in your life.

Femimundo Limited organizes the first international exhibition of woman and her world. Everything new that is produced in the country. Fashion and elegance, beauty, cosmetics, diet, articles for the home. Femimundo Limited, based on profound studies and experiences, organizes this show, directing its interests and appealing for the first time to the most powerful factor of consumption in today's world: woman.

Despite such self-serving claims of listening to and addressing women's needs, a performance of altruism and modernity that purports to bring about personal development—"Femimundo cambiará algo en su vida. Por eso, cuando usted salga de Femimundo, notará que algo muy suyo, muy íntimo habrá cambiado. Se habrá enriquecido" (Femimundo will change something in your life. That's why, when you leave Femimundo, you will notice that something very much yours, very intimate, will have changed)—Bemberg will quickly resignify this discourse to make it clear that the modern woman created is not an empowered subject but a woman who has responded to an imperative to transform herself into yet another object of consumption for men.

The opening of the film establishes its central motif through the Cinderella story, which Beauvoir herself had discussed as a persistent patriarchal myth that survives great historical shifts: "What determines women's present situation is the stubborn survival of the most ancient traditions in the new emerging civilization. . . . How could the Cinderella myth not retain its validity? Everything still encourages the girl to expect fortune and happiness from a 'Prince Charming' instead of attempting the difficult and uncertain conquest alone. . . . Parents still raise their daughters for marriage rather than promoting their personal development; and the daughter sees so many advantages that she desires it herself" (2011, 155). Despite the twentieth-century adventure of consumer modernity, cultural mediation of desire for girls falls into traditional models in which education and training emphasize less a capacity for action in the world than for self-regarding artifice, giving prime importance, that is, to physical appearance. As Beauvoir writes of fairy tales more generally, "The supreme necessity for woman is to charm a masculine heart; this is the recompense all heroines aspire to, even if they are intrepid, adventuresome; and only their beauty is asked of them in most cases. It is thus understandable that attention to her physical appearance can become a real obsession for the little girl; princesses or shepherds, one must always be pretty to conquer love and happiness; ugliness is cruelly associated with meanness, and when one sees the misfortunes that befall ugly girls, one does not know if it is their crimes or their disgrace that destiny punishes" (305). Such conflation of the physical with the moral, the inextricable connection between beauty and happiness, is, of course, not limited to fairy tales. It is the motor of the marketing strategies of the industry sectors that target women as consumers and, as such, the prime target of the critique in Bemberg's film. The found sound of a woman's voice opens the film, heard over black leader reading a Walt Disney version of *Cinderella*, a corporate rewriting that transforms it into an optimistic, consumer-friendly product devoid of the less seemly aspects of earlier versions (Tatar 101–104). In Disney's filmic versions of classic fairy tales, as Jack Zipes writes, "the young women are helpless ornaments in need of protection, and when it comes to the action of the film, they are omitted" (349). When the Disney narrator tells of the arrival of the invitation from the royal palace, images are seen of the Sociedad Rural in preparation for the exposition, being transformed into a fantasy palace of purchasing power and the freedom to choose among abundant consumer goods, all of which serve (according to their marketing claims) the unquestioned imperative of making women more attractive to men. When the narrator mentions the prince, a young, shirtless blond workman is seen preparing the stalls for the exhibition. As the film progresses, this initial man, a believable yet anachronistic Prince Charming type, will give way to the men who participate in the expo, a shift that transforms the motif of "man" from Prince Charming into a physically repulsive, openly scopophilic consumer of women.

Another main source of found material used in the film is the aforementioned women's magazine *Para Ti*, whose gender-traditionalist advice is read by a woman's voice-over:

> Debe ser romántica, generosa y poco exigente. . . . Debe ser sensual, pero no demasiado. Dele seguridad de que usted será una extraordinaria esposa. Como él, debe amar la música, la poesía, el hogar. . . . Sea apasionada cuando él lo quiera, pero no le pida lo mismo. Sea simple y genuina.

> You should be romantic, generous and not demanding. . . . You should be sensuous, but not too much so. Offer him security that you will be an extraordinary wife. Like him, you should love music, poetry, the home. . . . Be passionate when he desires it, but don't ask the same of him. Be simple and genuine.

Bemberg does not allow these pithy yet contradictory recommendations of self-abnegating immanence to stand, and relentlessly ironizes them through montage effects by juxtaposing them with images of young women connected to various modern body-shaping machines that appear to bear a curiously premodern capacity to inflict pain on the body. A likely synthesis derived from the associations created by this vertical montage is that instead of simple and genuine beings, women under patriarchy are plagued by insecurities so intense as to drive them to painful artifice to cling to the opportunity to catch and keep the eye of their Prince Charming.

Toward the film's end a rhythmic montage sequence generates an aesthetic supplement in the form of a visceral appeal that produces an effect characteristic of what Linda Williams refers to as the "body genres"—horror, melodrama, pornography—that "make the body do things" (Gaines 1999). But where the body genres produce screams, tears, and sexual arousal, *El mundo de la mujer*, in addition to a consciousness of the role played by modern consumerism in the subjugation of women, ideally intensifies the indignance that might spur the viewer to action against the oppressive assemblage of patriarchy and consumer culture. The accelerated rhythmic montage sequence consisting of images of the expo cut to music and accompanied first by a sequence of imperatives—"Debe ser romántica. Debe ser paciente. Debe ser sensual. Debe ser ordenada" (You must be romantic. You must be patient. You must be sensual. You must be well-ordered)—then by the also-rhythmic orgasmic cries of a woman (an eloquent testimony to the often-denied fact of female desire?), is abruptly halted. In a freeze-frame, one of the heavily made-up expo models peers through vertical elements that become, with the tight framing of the shot, the bars of a cell, accompanied by the now familiar voice narrating the happy ending of *Cinderella*, which can no longer be received as unproblematic bliss: "Ahí terminó la tarea del gran duque. Había encontrado la dueña del zapatito de cristal. La llevó al castillo, donde Cenicienta y el príncipe se casaron y fueron muy felices" (There ended the task of the Great Duke. He had found the owner of the glass slipper. He brought her to the castle, where Cinderella and the prince married and were very happy). Here the resignification of the palace motif reaches its conclusion as prison, and the Cinderella myth, as well as the advice offered by *Para Ti*, are suggested to be road maps to a life of soul-stifling servitude.

El mundo de la mujer was reedited later by Bemberg in the interest of making its politics appear less militant. Sara Torres, a fellow member of UFA who had appeared in the film passing out flyers, reports that the original film included a shot of the flyer itself in close-up, which is absent in the currently available copies. Bemberg's secretary at the time has recently said that after becoming established as a director of fiction features, Bemberg felt embarrassed by the militancy of her earlier films and possibly eliminated parts of them to soften the radicality of their politics (Trebisacce and Veiga 1409). But while the later Bemberg may not have expressed pride in *El mundo de la mujer*'s radicalism and the direct action depicted in the early version, a somewhat opposed yet more current critique of Bemberg's film might echo bell hooks's take on Betty Friedan's *Feminine Mystique*: the film could be considered a product of an insular gaze proper to a bourgeois feminism, and its disregard for the condition of those women who are not wealthy enough to participate in the consumer fairyland that is the Femimundo expo means that its concern and appeal are limited to an overprivileged minority of predominantly white, middle-class Argentine women. But an argument could also be made for the film's prescience, since enthrallment to consumerist femininity has, in the ensuing half century, gone far beyond being an exclusively middle-class privilege. As globalized finance capital chases ever-cheaper labor to produce commodities at the same time that it expands access to the credit economy, the market integrates more and more consumers and the conditions wrought by it are further universalized.

Juguetes, Bemberg's other short film, was shot at the Feria de Juguetes (Toy Fair) exposition, also at the Sociedad Rural, in 1977. Screened during the dictatorship, it is less aesthetically radical and more discursively didactic than *El mundo de la mujer*, and its distribution was more traditional.[25] It opens with texts that clearly state its thesis: "Desde la infancia las expectativas de conducta son distintas para cada sexo. Se educa a los hijos de manera específica para que actúen de manera específica. . . . Los juguetes y los cuentos no son inocentes: son la primera presión cultural" (From infancy on, behavior expectations are different for each sex. Children are educated in a specific way so that they act in a specific way. . . . Toys and stories are not innocent: they are the first cultural pressure). *Juguetes* goes on to examine the gender-normatizing role of children's culture, mostly through interviews with children in which an interviewer with microphone in hand asks, "¿Qué vas a ser cuando seas grande?" (What are you going to be when you grow up?). The boys and girls respond with the typical gender-appropriate choices, the former imagining for themselves futures as athletes, businessmen, or ship captains, while the latter mostly plan to go into teaching. In an interview, Bemberg held that this is an economic mistake, since it dooms the girls to dependency on a man: "In many cases they choose those careers, so badly remunerated, of teacher and nurse. Not doctors or professors. Stewardesses, but not pilots" ("María Luisa Bemberg y un film feminista" n. pag.). The final child, who is Bemberg's granddaughter, is a little girl walking hand in hand with her older brother (Fontana 22). She responds to the question by opening her jacket to reveal a shirt on which is printed her name, "BARBARA," a response that at the same time declares her uniqueness and rebels against the normatizing power of the discourse of civilization.[26]

Direction was not Bemberg's only participation in the cinema during the 1970s. She scripted two notable films made in the first half of the decade, *Crónica de una señora* (Chronicle of a woman, Raúl de la Torre, 1971) and *Triángulo de cuatro* (Triangle of four, Fernando Ayala, 1975). The protagonist of the former is Fina (played by Graciela Borges), the wife of a landowner (Lautaro Murúa). Fina's life "passes by between lunches at the Rural, polo matches and weekend strolls through the estancia" (V. García and Peña 89), but when she is suddenly thrust into a crisis after the unexpected suicide of a friend and fellow aristocrat, she begins to examine her situation as devoted housewife and mother. In a central episode of this "x-ray of the crisis of a class that could not permit itself any transformation" (90), when Fina reads *Le deuxième sexe* (in bed and in the original), she is interrupted in turns by the maid, the children's French nanny, and the phone. In frustration she turns off the ringer and commands the maid to tell any visitors she is not in. Fina's crisis and reading of Beauvoir lead her to conceive of her condition as imprisoned, isolated from society by her wealth and responsibilities. She takes steps to liberate herself, in part through an affair, but her triumph over bourgeois immanence is only apparent, and by the film's end she finds herself in the identical situation (even with the same lover) that drove her friend to suicide. As in Lah's films, the limitations imposed by the factic are felt all too materially. As Catherine Grant writes, the film "ends with a fade, nearly to black, which is also frozen, and a sudden burst of dissonant music immediately after this stilled image of Fina, emphasizing her entrapment in a situation or 'condition' which cannot be altered, it seems, simply by having more fulfilling adulterous affairs" (76).

Gender is the central concern of the film, but the inevitable consideration of the class dynamics of Fina's situation raises thorny questions, about both the film and Bemberg's own condition as a woman of stratospheric wealth. Are the interruptions of Fina's attempt to read *The Second Sex* a suggestion that the upper-class woman has too much on her plate to form herself intellectually? As seen elsewhere in Bemberg's work, an unspoken class envy seems to underlie the film. Fina wants to get a paying job—not as the owner of a gallery but as an employee—which seems to confirm, as Rita De Grandis writes, that Bemberg's "notable artistic participation was made possible and at the same time limited by her origin and class perspective . . . she was even naïve enough to think that a woman who worked had certain advantages as far as her freedom of self-affirmation due to being obligated to earn her own living" (4). Such ideological blind spots spurred critiques of Bemberg that resonate with disdain toward her class allegiance. In criticizing her as willfully blind to the horrors of the dictatorship, based on the two features she directed during that period, Eduardo Rojas writes that "while María Luisa Bemberg imprecisely told our stories, around us thousands of men and women were disappearing, torn from Argentine homes by the brutal impunity of the dictatorship. . . . These fictional women can repeat 'I didn't know' in chorus with thousands of men and women of Argentina who chose to not know of the horror of the dictatorship and assume a degree of complicity that the entire country has not yet compensated" (72). Rojas's equation of Bemberg's protagonists with such society-wide denial is a less than apposite comparison, since due to state control over the cinema under the dictatorship it was nearly impossible to reference the repression, and only a handful of filmmakers did so.[27] But an even more important omission in this line of critique is the failure to consider Bemberg's short films, since they make clear that her feminism is in direct resistance to the kind of retrograde cultural politics fomented by the previous military dictatorship, a position she maintains consistently throughout her features. Rather than accusations of complicity, a more well-grounded critique of Bemberg might limit itself to pointing out that her resistance is consistently defined and limited by her own class allegiance.

Continuity between her shorts and early features (both those she scripted and those she directed) can be seen in the centrality of the subjectivity of women who are deeply troubled after a process of conscientization puts them in tension with their situation as women in a patriarchal society. While the features always contain a protagonist who undergoes this process, in *El mundo de la mujer* the primary subject of conscientization is the viewer, wherein lies the greater militancy of the film. Such a conception allows us to formulate a clear political difference with respect to her features, which Estela Erausquin points to when she writes of the female characters in *Miss Mary* (1986) that "although suffering from repressed sexuality constitutes a link between women, the director does not envision a possible subversive sisterhood. As in her previous films, Bemberg lacks the intention of suggesting a conversion of this female unity in shame into a binding and revolutionary force. Had it been otherwise, the emphasis on similarities between women would have become explicit for the audience, if not for the characters, and her films would have become a subversive weapon" (55). Unlike in *Miss Mary* and other features, in *El mundo de la mujer* there are no such individualized protagonists who might block the binding of her viewers into such a sisterhood, and the female force prompted has no reason not to unify into a reciprocal project to demand social change.

More than a decade before Bemberg made her shorts, Lah's films had articulated incisive inquiries into the effects of the intersection of class and gender on the situation of women. Already in the 1970s, María Herminia Avellaneda and María Elena Walsh critiqued the effects of authoritarian politics on the gender order while, contemporary to Bemberg, Eva Landeck formulated both direct and indirect representations of state terror under the dictatorships. While Bemberg is deservedly considered one of the most important directors of Argentine cinema history, my hope is that this book might point to other optics through which to consider how she and other women managed to make films that articulated questions about women's condition. Such inquiries might encounter surprising connections between seemingly incompatible filmmakers, one of which is found at Bemberg's turn from scriptwriting to direction.

Bemberg made her short films after she had scripted *Crónica de una señora*. Her displeasure with the finished film led directly to her work as director, as John King explains: "In her view, [the director Raúl de la Torre] felt no sympathy for the woman protagonist, Fina, and her existential emptiness. She remarked on this to the director of photography, Juan Carlos Desanzo, who replied: 'Why don't you direct yourself?'" (16–17). Bemberg tells of her surprised reaction and eventual acceptance: "Me? . . . a woman? I know nothing about the technical side. Desanzo argued that all one needed was to know the basics and count on a good assistant director, a lighting technician and an editor. He was right, as Françoise Pasturier has said, *it's time for us women to dare to dare*. And I dared" (17). It is intriguing to consider a hidden link between Eva

Landeck and Bemberg that runs through Desanzo. Soon after working on *Crónica de una señora*, he worked under Landeck on *Gente en Buenos Aires*, which may have convinced him that women could direct successfully and articulate their own perspectives.

The films discussed in this chapter have been forgotten by Argentine film history, probably due less to any inherent bias by scholars than to an original lack of distribution and subsequent unavailability. This has changed. Since it is now possible to fill in the gaps in film history that led to the Bemberg of the 1980s being considered as the sole precursor of women directors and feminist film in Argentina, we can tell a far more complex story, one in which other women dared to direct, despite the many challenges.

Acknowledgments

Many individuals contributed directly and indirectly to this book. From my days as a graduate student: David Castillo, Kaja Silverman, Jeffrey Skoller, Natalia Brizuela, Ignacio Navarrete, Francine Masiello, Mia Fuller, Steven Botterill, Chris Eagle, Pablo Baler, Andrei Dubinsky, and others; and Steve Seid, Kathy Geritz, and everyone else at the Pacific Film Archive who make cinephilia happen. Especially valuable was the tireless support and generosity of Dru Dougherty.

Thanks to my colleagues at the University of Kentucky: Yanira Paz, Ana Rueda, Aníbal Biglieri, Haralambos Symeonidis, Alan Brown, Moisés Castillo, Carmen Moreno-Nuño, Dierdra Reber, Irene Chico-Wyatt, Heather Campbell-Speltz, Jorge Medina, Arcelia Gutiérrez, and Mónica Díaz.

Much appreciated is the support from Jens Andermann, Marvin D'Lugo, Ignacio Sánchez Prado, Geoffrey Kantaris, Gary Crowdus, Tamara Falicov, and especially David William Foster.

Infinite thanks to the librarians of the Biblioteca de la Escuela Nacional de Experimentación y Realización Cinematográfica in Buenos Aires, especially, but not only, Lucio Mafud and Adrián Muoyo for their generosity and knowledge, which make this kind of project possible. To Fabián Sancho of the Museo de Cine Pablo Ducrós Hicken for the same, and to those at the Biblioteca y Hemeroteca of the Museo Evita, the Instituto Nacional de Estudios de Teatro in Buenos Aires's Teatro Cervantes, the Biblioteca del Congreso de la Nación Argentina, and the Biblioteca de Argentores. All were very generous and made research in Buenos Aires a pleasure.

My sincere appreciation for those archivists and audiovisual preservationists who rescue, care for, and screen the cinematic past, and to the organizers of the many film cycles and other events that make Buenos Aires a heaven for cinephiles. Of these, Fernando Martín Peña deserves recognition and admiration for his dedication to searching out, preserving, and screening films.

Clara Kriger, Sonia Sasiaín, Alejandro Kelly Hopfenblatt, Javier Cossalter, María Aimaretti, Lucio Mafud, Pablo Piedras, Rocío Gordon, Martino Pereira, Andrea Cuarterolo, and many others in Argentina were generous with knowledge and materials.

Much love and appreciation to Gerardo, Carmita, Feña, Vale, Toni, Lucía, Micaela (!), Lola, Fernando Pampa, Tato, Fede (especially for conversations about film and help tracking down materials), Gabi, and Mizuko, and to Aunt Irene and my cousins.

Next to last is a shout-out to those lovers of literature, appreciators of art, and stemless students whose place in the university grows ever narrower and more underestimated. It's tough out there. Keep the faith and stay out of debt.

Saved for last is appreciation and love for my mother Patricia, Pops, and Mike; for Pepita (you're still missed); and the deepest love and gratitude to Remi and Mia, whose appearance in my life drew me toward this project, and to whom it is dedicated.

Filmography

Apollon musagète (1951). Dir. Irena Dodal.
Blanco y negro (1919). Dir. Elena Sansinena de Elizalde.
Come out (1971). Dir. Narcisa Hirsch.
Cómo se hace una película argentina (1948). Dir. Arturo Mom.
Crónica de una señora (1971). Dir. Raúl de la Torre. Script, María Luisa Bemberg.
De los abandonados (1962). Dir. Mabel Itzcovich.
El bombero está triste y llora (1965). Dirs. Lita Stantic and Pablo Szir.
El hambre oculta (1965). Dir. Dolly Pussi.
El lugar del humo (1979). Dir. Eva Landeck.
El mundo de la mujer (1972). Dir. María Luisa Bemberg,
Ese loco amor loco (1979). Dir. Eva Landeck.
Informes y testimonios: La tortura política en Argentina, 1966–1972 (1973). Dirs. Diego Eijo, Eduardo Giorello, Ricardo Moretti, Alfredo Oroz, Carlos Vallina, Silvia Verga.
Gente en Buenos Aires (1973). Dir. Eva Landeck.
Homecoming (1978). Dir. Narcisa Hirsch.
Juguemos en el mundo (1971). Dir. Eva Landeck.
Juguetes (1978). Dir. María Luisa Bemberg.
La fiancée du pirate (1969). Dir. Nelly Kaplan.
Las furias (1960). Dir. Vlasta Lah.
Las modelos (1963). Dir. Vlasta Lah.
Los taxis (1970). Dirs. Diego Eijo, Eduardo Giorello, Ricardo Moretti, Alfredo Oroz, Carlos Vallina, Silvia Verga.
Operativo Brigadier Estanislao López (1973). Dir. Dolly Pussi.

Negro sobre blanco (2004). Dir. Eduardo López.
Pescadores (1968). Dir. Dolly Pussi.
Playa Grande (1943). Dirs. Amanda Lucía Turquetto and Hector Bernabó.
Soy de aquí (1965). Dir. Mabel Itzcovich.
Taller (1975). Dir. Narcisa Hirsch.

Notes

Introduction

1. The term "celluloid ceiling" is used by Martha Lauzen to address the lack of opportunities for women in U.S. audiovisual production.
2. My use of the term "auteur" is aligned with that of Angela Martin, who emphasizes a filmmaker's marginal position relative to the film industry rather than a necessary filmic presence of a female voice.
3. The most notable exceptions to these conventional representations are seen in what Alejandro Kelly Hopfenblatt refers to as the "comedia de fiesta," especially in films made during the second half of the 1940s and after by Carlos Schlieper and by Carlos Hugo Christensen, in which the motivations of female characters "originate with the vitality of sexual desire at the same time that they call into question their roles in the family and society" (Kelly Hopfenblatt 87).
4. Ramírez Llorens studies the effects of Catholic pressure groups on Argentine cinema (2014, 2016, 2017).
5. I am referring to the use of mechanisms with which films prompt identification, which include narrative focalization and the representation of what Bordwell and Thompson describe as perceptual subjectivity and mental subjectivity (82–89).
6. The *primavera camporista* is a reference to the climate of revolutionary optimism and cultural opening around the presidency of Héctor Cámpora (May 25 to July 13, 1973).
7. Among the many women who have directed since, Clara Zappettini made the city essay *Buenos Aires, la tercera fundación* (1980) and Mercedes Frutos directed a fiction feature based on a short story by

Adolfo Bioy Casares, *Otra esperanza*, in 1984, though it was not screened until 1991 (Manrupe and Portela 436). Silvia Chanvillard and Laura Bua formed the group Cine Testimonio Mujer and made several short documentaries (Margulis 100), and Carmen Guarini has produced and directed many politically engaged documentaries since *Buenos Aires, crónicas villeras* (1988) and *La noche eterna* (1991) (102–107). Jeanine Meerapfel directed *Desembarcos* (1986–1989), a documentary on the postdictatorship, the features *La amiga* (1988) and *Amigomío* (1995), which engage with repressive violence and exile, as well as several films made in various parts of Europe. Ana Poliak directed *¡Que vivan los crotos!* (1990), a remarkable documentary feature on the memories and return home of the anarchist Bepo Ghezzi after sixty years of life as a nomadic *linyera*, which translates roughly as hobo. Lita Stantic made *Un muro de silencio* (1993), which is often cited as the most incisive postdictatorship film on the theme of memory. More recently, with the proliferation of the kind of creative funding strategies and less expensive production models pioneered by Poliak and Stantic, by the first decade of the twenty-first century several women had become established directors, and a decade later it has become difficult to count how many women have made films, many of them extremely successful both critically and commercially (Bettendorf and Pérez Rial 32–38; Margulis 107–112).

8. A final note on sources of the films discussed here: This book would not have been possible without the felicitous combination of the perseverance and generosity of archivists with the proliferation of digital technologies in the last couple of decades. As of this writing, few of the films exist in commercially available formats. Landeck's *Gente en Buenos Aires* was released on a DVD sold with her novel *Máscaras provisorias* (2016). Lita Stantic's two shorts, along with her sole feature, *Un muro de silencio*, were released on a DVD sold with Eseverri and Peña's book. Much of Narcisa Hirsch's work appeared on the DVD *El cine experimental de Narcisa Hirsch*. Her short *Come out* (1971) also appears on the DVD collection of experimental films *Cine a contracorriente*, edited in Spain. Most of the other films discussed, and some of the ones just mentioned, can be found on video-sharing websites or through informal sources. Since the

contents of these change rapidly, at times this requires some searching.

1. A History of the Gendered Division of Labor in Argentine Cinema

1. Hill explores these roles in great detail in the context of the Hollywood industry.
2. This dynamic will be familiar to scholars of silent film in the United States, where many women worked as directors and producers before the formation of the studios that would dominate production and relegate women to less creative "feminine labor" for several decades (Gaines 2018; Hill).
3. Mafud's account does not mention the founding of the production company, and thus mentions only Camila Quiroga's participation in the role of actress (2016, 279–282). He lists María B. de Celestini as a possible owner of Andes Films, the producer of the film she directed, *Mi derecho* (1920).
4. According to Fradinger, *El pañuelo de Clarita* has survived in private hands. She also cites reports of René Oro, who made a documentary titled *La Argentina* (1922) (2014 ["Women in Argentine Silent Cinema"], n. pag.).
5. Another film possibly directed by Saleny, according to Mafud, is *Luchas en la vida* (1919) (2016, 307).
6. Another very early film is *La caperucita blanca*, made in 1916 by Antonieta Capurro de Renauld. This film and a documentary, *La escuela para niños débiles del parque Lezama*, are described in the daily *La Razón*, as quoted by Mafud: "They form part of the material included in the didactic plan developed by said lady in the school for debilitated children of Parque Lezama, and which correspond to a campaign to introduce a special educational cinematograph, offered as a means of study and relaxation for the children of all the schools of the Republic" (qtd. in Mafud 2016, 161). Mafud also convincingly argues that María Constanza Bunge Guerrico de Zavalía should be credited with the direction of *Los cisnes encantados* (1919), a film that has previously been attributed to Francisco Defilippis Novoa (305).

7. Based on several articles in the press of the time, Mafud includes as codirectors Victoria Ocampo (who also acts in the film) and Adelia Acevedo (2016, 311).
8. Halperín Donghi provides a concise account of the Liga Patriótica in *Vida y muerte de la República verdadera (1919–1930)* (136–142).
9. Mafud finds that the authorship of the film is difficult to conclusively attribute to María B. de Celestini (2016, 329).
10. The creative roles played by women in the cinema's first two decades, as well as the subsequent absence of women in such roles in the classical studio cinema, are phenomena in no way limited to Argentina (Gaines 2004, 113).
11. In contrast to the previous decades, as Conde writes, "between 1933 and 1955, the industrial, technical and artistic production of the industrial sound cinema was a task of men" (2009, 185). Studies of the transition to industry in Hollywood offer intriguing parallels to the case of Argentina. Erin Hill describes a historical regression for women in Hollywood that seems to closely parallel that seen later in Argentina:

> Women's relatively high level of participation in the heterosocial workplaces of early film production began to shift in the late 1910s and early 1920s, with the "efficient" reorganization of studios and attendant sex segregation and feminization practices under which work was separated, classified, and relocated (as such) to accommodate the studios' aims. According to this logic, the largest feminized labor sector—that of clerical work—emerged as a key component of efficient mass production, facilitating expanded management and cost accounting, reducing labor costs, and absorbing mass film production's lowest-status, most repetitive, least desirable forms of labor on the basis that they were women's work. As it had elsewhere, efficiency shifted the film industry from less formal, more holistic early work systems in which women moved fluidly between different work sectors (presenting a kind of unintended or latent feminism), to a highly structured, rigid organizational model. (16–17)

Karen Ward Mahar focuses on the imposition by finance capital of "rational" methods of film production that excluded women from creative roles (179–208). Her description of the transition to industry in Hollywood emphasizes the gendered demands of finance capital:

> An unmistakable pattern emerged by the first decades of the twentieth century: big business, that is business with large capital requirements and national distribution, was masculine. "The search for order" was in fact a gendered search; rationalization and national distribution were freighted with gendered concepts that proved to be ultimately, but not immediately, unfavorable to women. When industries were small and decentralized, as the film industry was during the nickelodeon era, female entrepreneurs tended to abound. But as industries became larger, centralized, and dependent on outside capital, as did so many at the start of the twentieth century, work once defined as suitable for women was redefined as suitable only for men. (204)

12. Studies of the career trajectories of individual women who worked in the Argentine silent cinema have yet to be written, with the exception of Moira Fradinger's brief but extensively researched account of the career of Emilia Saleny (2014 ["Huellas de archivo"]). Nor has a history of distribution during the period (which might show at which point the more artisanal production had difficulty accessing audiences). Both of these might help elucidate the process of exclusion.

13. Pécora and Ortuno state that in the classical cinema industry "not a single woman occupied a role in the technical areas.... During that period women worked more or less systematically in costume design and art direction, tasks that were still considered minor in film production" (85). Bettendorf and Pérez Rial, in their brief but thorough account of women in film direction in Argentina, put it similarly: "Traditionally, within the strict division of labor imposed by the studio cinema . . . women had positions in the teams working on costumes and in the area of makeup, or they worked as negative cutters; only a very few made it to assistant director" (17–18).

14. Conde mentions Lina C. de Machinandiarena, the wife of the owner of Estudios San Miguel, and Paulina Singermann, a star actress who came to produce films in which she acted (2009, 189). Others, including Niní Marshall, Olga Casares Pearson, and Nené Cascallares, wrote scripts (186–187).

15. Hill expands on the role of the negative cutter as feminized labor (188–194).
16. In 1992 the Instituto Nacional de Cinematografía recognized Bróndolo with a prize for her career trajectory, which resulted in press attention and at least two published interviews, in *La Razón* and *La Nación*. In the first she comments on her long-term relegation to the role of negative cutter (M. García), yet the writer of the latter describes the job of negative cutter in essentialist terms, as "a job that, in its patience and delicateness, always demands a feminine hand attentive to the cut and the join of the films, assuming the highest responsibility, loving in the observation of each sequence" (Martínez, n. pag.).
17. See Daniel López (63–64) for a more extensive list of women who worked in the industry. As assistant directors he lists "Lucy Blanco and Chola Rossi in Establecimientos Filmadores Argentinos (EFA), Alicia Míguez Saavedra as freelancer, Vlasta Lah at Estudios San Miguel, Susana Gallup at Pampa Film and Rosa Blumkin at Artistas Argentinos Asociados (AAA)" (63).
18. Irena Dodal's time in Argentina remains little studied. The most authoritative account available is that of Strusková (315–332).
19. The catalog of the Centro de las Artes de Expresión Audiovisual (42) dates the film at 1960, but it was clearly made earlier.
20. Anchou traces the origin of several *cineclubes* and short filmmaking back to the early 1930s (404).
21. Aimaretti, Bordigoni, and Campo also briefly discuss *Feria franca*, but they spell its director's name differently, as "Hercilia" Marino (383), while Truglio spells it "Harcilia" Moreno (311).
22. Contardi, according to Beatriz Sarlo, was at the Instituto at the time when it was divided between *birristas*, those who followed Birri's mode of social documentary, and the *antibirristas*, or *estetistas*. She formed part of the latter group (227). She went into exile in France during the dictatorship, returned to Santa Fe in 1985, and helped found the Taller de Cine at the Universidad Nacional del Litoral. Meanwhile, she has had a fruitful career as a poet, professor, and maker of about twenty documentary films (Gigena n. pag.).
23. As of this writing all of Pussi's films of the 1960s and 1970s are available for viewing online.

24. These are of course the continents from which the next year would come the participants in the gathering in Havana of representatives of national liberation movements known as the Tricontinental Conference.
25. The continuation of this discourse reveals much about the strategies and rhetorical practice of a Juventud Peronista that during the Cámpora presidency was already locked into a violent struggle against the orthodox Peronism that would soon gain dominance of the movement after the return of Perón to the presidency:

> En este sentido el Operativo de Reconstrucción Nacional Brigadier General Estanislao López contempla dos aspectos. Por un lado, ir hacia nuestro norte, ir hacia los hombres de nuestro pueblo santafesino para llevarle nuestra solidaridad, para llevarle nuestro trabajo concreto y ayudarlos a paliar, aunque no nos sean parte, sus problemas. En ese sentido los compañeros de Juventud Peronista que lleven adelante este operativo cumplirán con tareas de construcción de ranchos, reparación de escuelas, hospitales, construcción de caminos, zanjeos, campañas sanitarias, campañas de vacunación masiva, etcetera. Y el otro aspecto del que hablábamos de este operativo es el aspecto político, el que será el poder mantener no solo a mil compañeros de Juventud Peronista movilizados, sino a gran parte de la población movilizada y organizándose para poder defender lo que se ha conseguido no gratuitamente sino con dieciocho años de lucha y poder asegurar de esa manera la reconstrucción y la liberación definitiva de nuestra patria y de su pueblo.

> In this sense the National Reconstruction Operation Brigadier General Estanislao López consists of two aspects. On the one hand, to go to our north, toward those men of our Santa Fe pueblo to bring them our solidarity, to bring them our specific work and help them to alleviate their problems, even if they are not ours. In this way the compañeros of the Peronist Youth who carry out this operation will perform housing construction, repair of schools, hospitals, road work, trenching, health campaigns, mass vaccination campaigns, et cetera. And the other aspect of this operation of which we spoke is the political aspect, that which will allow us to keep mobilized not only a thousand compañeros of the Peronist Youth, but also a large

part of the population mobilized and organizing itself to be able to defend what has been accomplished not easily but through eighteen years of struggle and thus be able to ensure the reconstruction and definitive liberation of our homeland and its pueblo.

26. Obeid went on to a long career in Peronist politics, including as governor of Santa Fe province from 2003 to 2007 (Ciucci).

27. Women studied film at La Plata as early as 1960. In a list compiled by Fernando Martín Peña of films produced in the program, the names of the following women appear as "collaborators": Nanda Frati, Sara Iturría, Angela María Nigri, Nelva Braviz López, Marta Gersanik, Clara Zappettini, Sara Krell, Diana Ferraro, Celia Birón, Agustina Risuod, Hilda Vizcarra Tamayo, Marilyn Rousiot, Gloria Martínez, and Nora Zapico (2006, 45–89).

28. Pompeya is a working-class neighborhood in southern Buenos Aires.

29. Other filmmakers for whom brief mentions can be found in catalogs and the press from the 1960s and 1970s are Mercedes D'Adderio, who in 1969 directed, on 16 millimeter, the fiction short *Desayuno*, based on a poem by Jacques Prevert ("Corto argentino premiado" 510); Nora Susana Stagnaro, who directed *Retrato a un pintor: Forte* ("Dieron los premios"); and Fabienne Rousso-Lenir, who is mentioned, in a brief article in *La Nación*, as being an Argentine director of a short, *La casa del río* (1973), that participated in a festival in France ("El Festival de Cortometraje"). Mercedes Frutos made *Calcomanías* (1979), in which "with a duration of six minutes, the story is told of an eleven-year-old boy who sends a letter to his grandfather" ("Asociación de cortometrajistas" n. pag.). In 1984 she would direct the feature *Otra esperanza*, which did not premiere until 1991 (Manrupe and Portela 436). Paulina Fernández Jurado worked in film criticism and exhibition from the early 1960s, headed the Centro de Investigaciones de la Historia del Cine Argentino, and served as long-term director of the Fundación Cinemateca Argentina (Sammaritano 1962 ["Diccionario de la nueva generación argentina"], 5–6). She also worked in various capacities in film production and directed at least two shorts, *El cartero* (1962) and *Mujeres* (1966) (Dimitriu; Bettendorf and Pérez Rial 22–23).

30. Alemann, who also participated in the Grupo Goethe, was an early collaborator of Hirsch on her films of the late 1960s. She made

experimental shorts in the 1970s and 1980s. In the area of experimental film, Laura Abel (Honik) also merits a mention for her codirection (with Jorge Honik) of the Super 8 short *Passacaglia y fuga* (1975).

31. In the 1990s, Silvestre Byrón wrote of experimental cinema as a fourth cinema, setting it in contrast with what Noël Burch called the "Institutional Mode of Representation," describing it instead as an "optional mode of representation," "where the image is 'entranced,' with no predetermined destination, an object of interest in and of itself. Left to its optionality, the OMR privileges the 'is' of the image over the 'ought to be' of the IMR" (192).

32. These earlier films include *Marabunta* (1967), *Retrato* (1968), *Manzanas* (1968), and *Celebración* (1968) (Giunta 2018, 116–123).

33. A DVD containing much of Hirsch's work, *El cine experimental de Narcisa Hirsch*, was released in 2013 in Argentina. In recent years her films have been shown in retrospectives in, among other places, Buenos Aires (2012), Vienna (2012), Toronto (2013), San Francisco (2014), and Los Angeles (2018).

34. The name of Luis Brandoni, the male lead in Eva Landeck's *Gente en Buenos Aires*, appears among the many on the dictatorship's recently released (in 2013) secret blacklist of April 6, 1979, under the category "Fórmula 4," which is defined as "shows a Marxist ideological history that renders advisable their non-admittance and/or permanence in public administration, do not offer collaboration" ("Los nombres prohibidos" n. pag.). In practice this meant that those on the list could not find work in Argentina in either state or private productions. Some other important figures of the cinema found on the list are Alfredo Alcón, Héctor Alterio, Norman Briski, Leonardo Favio, Delia Garcés, Octavio Getino, Cipe Lincovsky, Federico Luppi, Duilio Marzio, Bárbara Mujica, Lautaro Murúa, Luis Politti, Marilina Ross, Pino Solanas, and María Vaner.

2. Eva Landeck

1. Clear examples of this apparent goodwill on the part of Perón are two films, *Perón: La revolución justicialista* (Perón: The Justicialist Revolution) and *Perón: Actualización política y doctrinaria para la toma del poder*

(Perón: Political and doctrinary update for the taking of power), made in 1971 by Fernando Solanas and Octavio Getino, in which the general lays out a strategy to prolong the movement through a passing of the Peronist torch through what he calls *trasvasamiento generacional* (generational transference).

2. On the delayed premiere Landeck recounts:
> We were assigned the Cine Iguazú. But *La tregua* had a powerful producer. When they sent *La tregua* instead of *Gente en Buenos Aires* to the Iguazú, I asked the distributor what happened. They told me to go see the owner of the Cine Monumental, whose children had spoken well to him of *Gente en Buenos Aires*. "And why do *I* have to go? You're the distributors." Even so, annoyed, I went. And I'm a bit shy, and was even more shy then. The owner of the Monumental, which was a big, important theater, met me and gave me a premiere date. . . . Finally they screened it. But it was on for four weeks and, although it was drawing enough spectators, they took it down. They sent it to the Lorraine. When they took it down there . . . I went to talk to Soffici, who was the director of the Institute [and] he had me sign a letter of official protest. Then a case was opened in my name. I went back to the Lorraine and they told me to go talk to Tato. "It's over for me," I thought. After that I received threats and they told me they rejected the case because the distributor had to file it, not me. Then I had to leave the country. (Hardouin and Ivachow 49–50)

3. The box office totals published in the *Heraldo del Cinematografista* confirm Landeck's memory: the film showed from the last week of August through the first week of October.

4. For his part, Brandoni mentions the threats but tells a slightly different story, speaking of a longer-term effort by the theater owner to replace the film with a foreign blockbuster: "*Gente en Buenos Aires* was relatively successful. I remember it opened at the Cine Monumental, . . . they screened it convinced that they'd get it off their backs after a week. But no. The second week they were definitely convinced that they'd move on to another film the next week. But no. . . . It stayed up for a third week and of course it couldn't take the pressure from the distributors

any longer. That's the crime that still happens today, although the method is more sophisticated" (Garcete n. pag.).

5. *Gente en Buenos Aires* has become more visible after being shown on Argentine television and occasionally in film club venues, and in 2016 a DVD of the film was published together with Landeck's novel *Máscaras provisorias*.

6. Mestman and Peña discuss the use of footage of the Cordobazo in several militant films and its meaning in relation to the differing ideological orientations of the makers of these.

7. The song is "El arriero" (alternatively "El arriero va"). The entirety of the fragment quoted is "Las penas y las vacas se van por la misma senda. Las penas son de nosotros, las vaquitas son ajenas" (The hardships and the cows travel the same road. The hardships are ours, the cows belong to others).

8. Militant narrative film depicted such practices in, for example, Gleyzer's *Los traidores* (1973) and Fernando Solanas's *Los hijos de Fierro* (1975).

9. There are exceptions, such as David José Kohon's short *Buenos Aires* (1958), which explores the relationship between the *villa miseria* and the city center by way of montage, Lautaro Murúa's *Shunko* (1960), and Fernando Birri's *Tire dié* (1956–1960) and *Los inundados* (1961). The Generación del 60 directors would explore the social margins in more depth toward the end of the decade and into the 1970s, with films like *Breve cielo* (David José Kohon, 1969) and *La Raulito* (Lautaro Murúa, 1975).

10. A film that contains clear references to the violence of groups like the Triple A is David José Kohon's *¿Qué es el otoño?* (1977). The protagonist witnesses a murder on the street by a death squad, and later a friend, an outspoken leftist professor, is murdered in a similar way. Varea, however, argues that there are certain concessions to censorship in Kohon's film (34–35).

11. *Ese loco amor loco* opened near the bottom of the box office chart (which appears in the *Heraldo del Cinematografista* that covers the week of September 27 to October 3, 1979) and did not stay on screen into the second week.

12. Gociol and Invernizzi provide a list of all ratings given to Argentine films under the dictatorship (81–89).

3. Beauvoir before Bemberg

1. Between these two publications, other work by Beauvoir was published in Argentina. The novel *Todos los hombres son mortales* was published in 1951 (by Emece) and *La invitada* in 1953 (Emece). Subsequent publications in the 1950s include *La sangre de los otros* (1955, Schapire), *Las bocas inútiles* (1957, Ariadna), and *Los mandarines* (1958, Sudamericana).
2. Julio Azamor summarizes the opinions of critics on Lah's two films: "According to the specialized critics, in these attempts, whose scripts are by Lah, she does not produce a feminine gaze on the problem of woman, perhaps because she does not have the opportunity to develop one, because of the scarcity of her production, or possibly because the public is not prepared to accept products of those characteristics, since the market conditions its themes and their treatments" (15).
3. The published information is contradictory, but in a personal interview the historian Martino Pereira, who is making a documentary on the filmmaker, informed me that Lah died in Buenos Aires in 1979.
4. Daniel López puts Lah's study at the Scuola Nazionale in doubt by recourse to the list of alumni on the website of the Centro Sperimentale, in which, he reports, Lah's name does not appear (64).
5. The list of professors includes women in "drawing and history of costumes, Nélida Lauría, . . . respiratory training and voice projection, Sara César, . . . rhythmic dance, Beatriz Ferrari, and folkloric dance, Angelita Vélez" ("Escuela de Cine Inicia Clases" 192).
6. The only mentions of the school I have been able to locate are in *Heraldo del Cinematografista* on the dates of July 21, August 4, October 6, and November 10, 1954, and June 15 and July 6, 1955.
7. *Las furias* was shown in 2014 at the Museo de Arte Latinoamericano de Buenos Aires in the cycle *Misterios de la Filmoteca*, organized by Fernando Martín Peña.
8. In 1964, Tirso would publish Renato Pellegrini's novel *Asfalto*, which was temporarily banned for obscenity (Brant 120).

9. I borrow the term "homonegative" from Herbert J. Brant, who uses it to describe mid-twentieth-century Argentine culture. Brant uses the term in opposition to "homophobic" "in order to draw a distinction between the way homosexuality is viewed in Hispanic and (Northern) Euro-American cultures" (131).
10. While not the norm, films with female narrative focalizers certainly form part of the Argentine tradition. The prolific director Manuel Romero is an often-mentioned example, for films like *Mujeres que trabajan* (1938) and *Isabelita* (1940), among others.
11. Kruks writes about Beauvoir's "independent woman" that she "is the new professional woman, who has no need of a man to support her. In some ways she is the harbinger of the free woman of the future" (106).
12. The archives both of the Biblioteca del Instituto Nacional de Estudios de Teatro in Buenos Aires's Teatro Nacional Cervantes and of the Sociedad General de Autores de la Argentina (Argentores) list Suárez de Deza's play *Las furias* in their catalogs, but as of 2018 the text of the play was no longer found on their shelves.
13. In Argentina, the facticity of the institution of marriage was particularly rigid due to restrictive divorce laws. Before 1954, in order to divorce, one of the parties had to be found guilty of incompliance with conjugal obligations, but those who were divorced could not remarry. Under Perón, in 1954, a law was enacted that allowed the divorced to remarry, but after his overthrow this law was suspended by the de facto government. In 1968 the law authorized separation by mutual agreement, which avoided the need to establish blame on either party, but without the possibility of those divorced then marrying someone else; only in 1987 was the law changed to allow for divorce without mutual consent (Cosse 2010).
14. Elsa Daniel had also appeared in Torre Nilsson's *Graciela* (1956) and *La caída* (1959) and would appear in more of the director's films.
15. The term "moral compensation" was coined in the U.S. context by Joseph I. Breen, the enforcer of the Hays Code as chief of the Production Code Administration from 1934 to 1954. In addition to policing images and words that might be considered corrupting to Catholic eyes and ears, Breen's job was to ensure that Hollywood's films were morally edifying. Under the notion of moral compensation, "any theme

must contain at least sufficient good in the story to compensate for, and to counteract, any evil which it relates" (Doherty 11). Argentina's classical cinema industry also faced pressure from the state and Catholic groups, and employed a similar mechanism of moral compensation (Ramírez Llorens 2016, 2017).

16. After the isolated experience of Vlasta Lah, in Argentina no women made feature-length films in the 1960s. In the late 1960s the Argentine Nelly Kaplan made *La fiancée du pirate* (*A Very Curious Girl*), her first film of a long career in France. Having left Argentina definitively for France in 1952, at about twenty years of age, Kaplan developed friendships with Abel Gance, André Breton, Philippe Soupault, and other figures of French avant-garde culture of the first half of the century. She has integrated surrealist and feminist tenets into her filmmaking and writing over nine documentary films, six narrative features, and six novels (Colaux 158–159).

Despite her origins, Kaplan is universally referred to as a French filmmaker, having managed to insert herself fully in the French cultural field, and the few films of hers I have seen contain no references that I know of to her country of birth. This work might best be described as a feminist surrealism, in that its radical questioning of social institutions is based primarily on their role in the subjugation of women and the repression of their sexuality. Her relationship with Argentina—which she describes as a "une situation aberrante: être une femme dans une société sud-americaine" (an aberrant situation: to be a woman in a South American society) (Colaux 109)—and its cinema could be considered as comprising a negative image in her work, since the films she made in France are impossible to imagine being made or exhibited within the field of Argentine cinema of their time.

Chris Holmlund writes of her films and novels that "while Kaplan makes surrealist desires her own, fancifully portraying sexual acts like consensual incest and necrophilia which many find shocking, she challenges male surrealist authority by insisting on women's autonomy and by subverting sexist images, including those which are most flattering to women" (354). Geetha Ramanathan expands incisively on this point when she writes that Kaplan's "assumption that the erotic uses of visual excess can actually empower women, a point of view closer to third-wave feminists than might be apparent from the date of this film, 1969 . . . . [*La fiancée du pirate*] promises that feminist authority can be accrued by the use of the erotic without devaluing women or participating in commodity fetishism" (31–32).

17. See Montaldo or Sorensen Goodrich for historical accounts of *criollismo*.

18. Near the end of the film, in Bambuco's "laboratorio de burbujas electrónicas" (laboratory of electronic bubbles), the creations of Gyula Kosice are seen. A modernist Argentine artist, Kosice was cofounder of the avant-garde Madí group.

19. In the creative roles played by women in *Juguemos en el mundo*, Laraschi and Sibbald see the film as a precursor: "The first and only experience of María Elena Walsh in the cinema was in fact a precursor of feminine creation: writer, scriptwriter, composer, producer and actor in the first film produced by women in Argentina: *Juguemos en el mundo* (1971) never achieved wide distribution" (178).

20. Maranghello includes a concise account of *Juguemos en el mundo*: "As for the children's genre, *Juguemos en el mundo* (1971) was the first feature by María Herminia Avellaneda, with story and songs by María Elena Walsh. Doña Disparate and Bambuco leave Buenos Aires to live in a small town, looking for bucolic peace. Poetically humorous and creatively fertile, it featured a great cast and songs by Walsh that, strangely, slowed down the rhythm of the musical comedy" (190).

21. Bemberg's early shorts were not precarious in terms of funding. Besides Bemberg's own wealth, *Juguetes* was produced by the Tita Tamames and Rosa Zemborain, who had produced Sergio Renán's *La tregua* several years earlier.

22. Contemporary recognitions of similar awakenings were many. Another is that of Adrienne Rich, who wrote in the early seventies, in "When We Dead Awaken: Writing as Re-vision," that "in the last few years the women's movement has drawn inescapable and illuminating connections between our sexual lives and our political institutions. The sleepwalkers are coming awake, and for the first time this awakening has a collective reality; it is no longer such a lonely thing to open one's eyes" (1980, 35).

23. One revealing indication of the persistence of a categorical distinction between feminism and "politics" in Argentina is the lack of attention to Bemberg's work in the 1,226 pages of the two-volume *Historia del cine político y social en Argentina*, edited by Ana Laura Lusnich and Pablo Piedras. Attention to Bemberg is limited to three mentions of her films in passing, none of which goes into depth, though the omission is understandable when Argentine history and her class perspective are taken into account.
24. The film's thesis is summed up by Catalina Trebisacce: the "construction of woman for the consumption of man presupposes an absence of feminine desire and pleasure, or more concretely, it implies the production of a female pleasure mediated by male pleasure. Women desire for themselves what men desire in them" (23).
25. While I have been unable to find mentions in the press of *El mundo de la mujer*, private screenings of *Juguetes* were covered by several major publications, including the wide-circulation newspaper *Clarín*. The attendees were "less from the artistic world than from high society and advertising" ("Juguetes y Whisky") and very conspicuously included Bernardo Neustadt, the politically influential, conservative television journalist. The film also screened in the United States and Spain ("Juguetes en New York").
26. At precisely the halfway point of the film, a voice-over reads a quote from Simone de Beauvoir: "Cada vez que una mujer se comporta como un ser humano, se dice que imita al varón" (Each time a woman behaves as a human being, it is said she is imitating man).
27. Certain feature films made under the dictatorship did manage to represent the repressive violence or its consequences, like David José Kohon's *¿Qué es el otoño?* (1977), Adolfo Aristarain's *Tiempo de revancha* (1981), and, as seen in chapter 2, Eva Landeck's *Ese loco amor loco* (1979).

Works Cited

Aguilar, Gonzalo. *Otros mundos: Un ensayo sobre el nuevo cine argentino.* Buenos Aires: Santiago Arcos, 2006.

Aimaretti, María, Lorena Bordigoni, and Javier Campo. "La Escuela Documental de Santa Fe: Un ciempiés que camina." In *Una historia del cine político y social en Argentina (1896–1969)*, edited by Ana Laura Lusnich and Pablo Piedras. Buenos Aires: Nueva Librería, 2009: 359–394.

Amado, Ana. "Conflictos ideológicos, inscripciones textuales. El espacio doméstico en los melodramas fílmicos y literarios de los 50." In *Cine Argentino. Modernidad y vanguardias 1957/1983.* Vol. 1, edited by Claudio España. Buenos Aires: Fondo Nacional de la Cultura, 2005: 356–363.

Anchou, Gregorio. "Perfil de una nueva actitud." *Cine argentino: Modernidad y vanguardias, 1957/1983.* Vol. 1., edited by Claudio España. Buenos Aires: Fondo Nacional de las Artes, 2005: 404–419.

André, María Claudia. "Simone's Daughters: Beauvoir's Influence in the Works of Latin-American Women Writers." *Simone de Beauvoir Studies* 18 (2001–2002): 107–120.

Andrew, Barbara S. "Beauvoir's Place in Philosophical Thought." In *The Cambridge Companion to Simone de Beauvoir*, edited by Claudia Card. Cambridge: Cambridge UP, 2006: 24–44.

Andújar, Andrea. "Prólogo." *Historia, género y política en los '70.* Edited by Andrea Andújar, Nora Domínguez, and María Inés Rodríguez. Buenos Aires: Feminaria Editora, 2005: 11–16.

Andújar, Andrea, et al. "Prólogo." In *De minifaldas, militancias y revoluciones. Exploraciones sobre los 70 en la Argentina*, edited by

Andrea Andujar et al., Buenos Aires: Ediciones Luxemburg, 2009: 9–16.

"Asociación de Cortometrajistas. Pese a todo, aún hacen cine." *Convicción*, October 16, 1979.

Azamor, Julio. "Vlasta Lah." In *Diccionario del Cine Iberoamericano*, edited by Emilio Casares Rodicio. Madrid: Sociedad General de Autores y Editores/Fundación Autor, 2011: 15.

Banks, Miranda J. "Gender Below-the-Line: Defining Feminist Production Studies." In *Production Studies: Cultural Studies of Media Industries*, edited by Vicki Mayer, Miranda J. Banks, and John T. Caldwell. New York: Routledge, 2009: 87–98.

Beauvoir, Simone de. *The Ethics of Ambiguity*. Translated by Bernard Frechtman. New York: Open Road Integrated Media, 2015.

———. *Le deuxième sexe II, L'expérience vécue*. Paris: Gallimard, 1949.

———. *The Second Sex*. Translated by Constance Borde and Sheila Malovany-Chevallier. New York: Vintage Books, 2011.

Bergoffen, Debra B. *The Philosophy of Simone de Beauvoir: Gendered Phenomenologies, Erotic Generosities*. Albany: SUNY Press, 1996.

Bernini, Emilio. "Bello experimental y visión total en Narcisa Hirsch." In *El cine experimental de Narcisa Hirsch*, edited by Victoria Sayago. Buenos Aires: MQ2* editora, 2013: 10–17.

———. "Crítica política y continuidad estética: El cine argentino durante el terrorismo de Estado y la democracia (1976–1985)." *Romanische Studien* 3, no. 6 (2017): 57–77.

Bettendorf, Paulina, and Agustina Pérez Rial. "Cartografiando miradas. Mujeres que hacen cine en Argentina." In *Tránsitos de la mirada: Mujeres que hacen cine*, edited by Paulina Bettendorf and Agustina Pérez Rial. Buenos Aires: Libraria, 2014: 15–40.

Birri, Fernando. *La escuela documental de Santa Fe*. Rosario: Prohistoria, 2008.

Boland, Elisa. "Coloquio del disparate." In María Elena Walsh, *Doña Disparate y Bambuco*. Buenos Aires: Alfaguara, 2008: 72–73.

Bordwell, David, and Kristen Thompson. *Film Art: An Introduction*. 7th ed. New York: McGraw-Hill, 2004.

Brant, Herbert J. "Homosexual Desire and Existential Alienation in Renato Pellegrini's *Asfalto*." *Confluencia* 20, no. 1 (Fall 2004): 120–133.

Burucúa, Constanza. "Lita Stantic: Auteur Producer/Producer of Auteurs." In *Beyond the Bottom Line: The Producer in Film and Television*, edited by Andrew Spicer, A. T. McKenna, and Christopher Meir. New York: Bloomsbury, 2014: 215–228.

Butler, Alison. *Women's Cinema: The Contested Screen*. London: Wallflower, 2002.

Butler, Judith. "Beauvoir on Sade: Making Sexuality into an Ethic." In *The Cambridge Companion to Simone de Beauvoir*, edited by Claudia Card. Cambridge: Cambridge UP, 2006: 168–188.

Byrón, Silvestre. "MRO." In *Ism Ism Ism: Experimental Cinema in Latin America*, edited by Jesse Lerner and Luciano Piazza. Oakland: U California P, 2017: 190–203.

Caldini, Claudio. "Una nueva etapa en la historia del cine." In *Claudio Caldini: Experimental Films 1975–1982*, edited by Leandro Villaro. New York: Antennae Collection, 2012: 31–32.

Calveiro, Pilar. *Política y/o violencia: Una aproximación a la guerrilla de los años setenta*. Buenos Aires: Siglo Veintiuno Editores, 2013.

———. *Poder y desaparición: Los campos de concentración en Argentina*. Buenos Aires: Colihue, 1998.

Campo, Javier. *Cine documental argentino: Entre el arte, la cultura y la política*. Buenos Aires: Imago Mundi, 2012.

Campodónico, Raúl Horacio. *Trincheras de celuloide: Bases para una Historia Político-Económico del Cine Argentino*. Madrid: Fundación Autor, 2005.

Castillo, Alejandra. *Simone de Beauvoir: Filósofa, antifilósofa*. Buenos Aires: Ediciones La Cebra, 2017.

Cattaruzza, Alejandro. *Historia de la Argentina, 1916–1955*. Buenos Aires: Siglo Veintiuno Editores, 2016.

Centro de las Artes de Expresión Audiovisual, Instituto Torcuato Di Tella. *Cine Corto Argentino 1958/1964*. Buenos Aires: Instituto Torcuato Di Tella, 1964.

Cine club Núcleo. *Exhibición no. 231*, November 9, 1958.

———. *Exhibiciónes nos. 255 y 256*, April 27, 1959.

Ciucci, Juan. "Entrevista a Dolly Pussi." *Tierra en Trance* 13 (June 2014). Web.

Colaux, Denys-Louis. *Nelly Kaplan, Portrait d'une Flibustière*. Paris: Dreamland, 2002.

Conde, Mariana Inés. "Cine argentino y género femenino: Un asunto que no es de polleras." *III Jornadas de Jóvenes Investigadores*. Universidad de Buenos Aires. Instituto de Investigaciones Gino Germani. 2005. Web.

———. "Martes, día de damas: Mujeres y cine en la Argentina, 1933–1955." PhD diss., U de Buenos Aires, 2009.

"Corto argentino premiado." *Heraldo del Cine*, August 5, 1970, 510.

Cossalter, Javier. "El Fondo Nacional de las Artes y el cortometraje argentino. Modernización cultural y estética." *Sociohistórica* 40 (2017): 1–22.

———. "Renovación estética e instrumentalización política radical: El cortometraje moderno en la Argentina (1955–1976)." *Questión. Revista Especializada en Periodismo y Comunicación* 1, no. 47 (July–September 2015): 309–324.

Cosse, Isabella. "Los nuevos prototipos femeninos en los años 60 y 70: De la mujer doméstica a la joven 'liberada.'" In *De minifaldas, militancias y revoluciones: Exploraciones sobre los 70 en la Argentina*, edited by Andrea Andújar et al. Buenos Aires: Ediciones Luxemburg, 2009: 171–186.

———. "Una cultura divorcista en un país sin divorcio: La Argentina de 1956 a 1975." In *Los '60 de otra manera: Vida cotidiana, género y sexualidades en la Argentina*, edited by Isabella Cosse et al. Buenos Aires: Prometeo, 2010: 131–168.

De Grandis, Rita. "Introducción: María Luisa Bemberg o las trampas de la clase." *Revista Canadiense de Estudios Hispánicos* 26, no. 1 (2002): 3–14.

Denegri, Andrés. "El Grupo Goethe: Epicentro del cine experimental argentino." In *Territorios audiovisuales*, edited by Jorge La Ferla and Sofía Reynal. Buenos Aires: Libraria, 2012: 86–103.

Di Cola, Flavio. "Silvia Oroz, ou o cinema de lágrimas que explica o amor e dá sentido à vida." *Dossié: A Cidade e as Questões do Urbano* 1, no. 1 (2015): 209–219.

"Dieron los premios en el IV Festival del Film de Arte." *La Nación*, June 3, 1971.

Dimitriu, Christian. "Paulina Fernández Jurado (1926–2004)." *Journal of Film Preservation* 68 (December 2004). Web.

Di Núbila, Domingo. *La época de oro. Historia del cine argentino I*. Buenos Aires: Ediciones del Jilguero, 1998.

Doherty, Thomas. *Pre-Code Hollywood: Sex, Immorality and Insurrection in American Cinema, 1930–1934*. New York: Columbia UP, 1999.

Dorsky, Nathaniel. *Devotional Cinema*. Berkeley: Tuumba Press, 2003.

"El Festival de Cortometraje en Grenoble." *La Nación*, February 2, 1973, n. pag.

Erausquin, Estela. "María Luisa Bemberg's Revolt." *Revista Canadiense de Estudios Hispánicos* 26, no. 1 (2002): 45–57.

"Escasa fortuna de un Debut." *Correo de la Tarde*, November 4, 1960, n. pag.

"Escuela de Cine Inicia Clases en Septiembre." *Heraldo del Cinematografista*, August 4, 1954, 192.

Eseverri, Máximo, and Fernando Martín Peña. *Lita Stantic: El cine es automóvil y poema*. Buenos Aires: Eudeba, 2013.

España, Claudio. "Eva Landeck expone sus ideas y su tema." *La Opinión*, August 23, 1977, 20.

"Eva Landeck: Gente en Buenos Aires." *Filmar y Ver* 7 (n.d. [1974?]): 20–21.

"Eva Landeck inició el rodaje de su segundo film como directora." *La Opinión*, October 9, 1977.

Fabbro, Gabriela. "Lumiton, el berretín del cine." In *Cine argentino: Industria y clasicismo, 1933/1956*. Vol. 1, edited by Claudio España. Buenos Aires: Fondo Nacional de las Artes, 2000: 222–249.

"Falleció la crítica y cineasta Mabel Itzcovich." *La Nación*, June 1 2004.

"Fantasía y realidad en el filme de Eva Landeck." *La Nación*, September 28, 1979.

Félix-Didier, Paula. "Introducción." In *60/90 Generaciones*, edited by Fernando Martín Peña. Buenos Aires: MALBA, 2003: 11–21.

———. "La crítica de cine en los 60." In *60/90 Generaciones*, edited by Fernando Martín Peña. Buenos Aires: MALBA, 2003: 328–335.

Firestone, Shulamith. *The Dialectic of Sex: The Case for a Feminist Revolution*. New York: Farrar, Straus and Giroux, 1970.

Fondo Nacional de las Artes. *Cineteca*. Buenos Aires: Ministerio de Cultura y Educación, n.d.

———. *Quinta Festival Argentino del Film de Arte: Catálogo de las Películas Participantes*. Buenos Aires: Ministerio de Cultura y Educación, 1973.

Fontana, Clara. *María Luisa Bemberg*. Buenos Aires: Centro Editor de América Latina, 1993.

Forcinito, Ana. "'Óyeme con los ojos.' Miradas y voces en el cine de María Luisa Bemberg." In *Tránsitos de la mirada: Mujeres que hacen cine*, edited by Paulina Bettendorf and Agustina Pérez Rial, eds. Buenos Aires: Libraria, 2014: 41–68.

Fradinger, Moira. "Emilia Saleny." In *Women Film Pioneers Project*, edited by Jane M. Gaines, Radha Vatsal, and Monica Dall'Asta. Center for Digital Research and Scholarship. New York, NY: Columbia University Libraries, 2014. Web. Accessed May 9, 2014.

———. "Huellas de archivo al rescate de una pionera del cine sudamericano: Josefina Emilia Saleny (1894–1978)." *Cinémas d'Amérique Latine* 22 (2014): 12–23. Web.

———. "Women in Argentine Silent Cinema." In *Women Film Pioneers Project*, edited by Jane M. Gaines, Radha Vatsal, and Monica Dall'Asta. Center for Digital Research and Scholarship. New York, NY: Columbia University Libraries, 2014. Web. Accessed May 9, 2014.

Franco, Marina. "Anticomunismo, subversión y patria: Construcciones culturales e ideológicas en la Argentina de los 70." In *La guerra fría cultural en América Latina*, edited by Benedetta Calandra and Marina Franco. Buenos Aires: Biblos, 2012: 195–210.

Gaines, Jane M. "Film History and the Two Presents of Feminist Film History." *Cinema Journal* 44, no. 1 (Fall 2004): 113–119.

———. *Pink-Slipped: What Happened to Women in the Silent Film Industries?* Chicago: U of Illinois P, 2018.

———. "Political Mimesis." In *Collecting Visible Evidence*, edited by Gaines and Michael Renov. Minnesota: U Minnesota P, 1999: 84–102.

Garcete, Horacio. "Luis Brandoni: Entrevista." *Esto No Es Una Revista*, n.d. Web. Accessed October 20, 2013.

García, Marcelo. "Prisionera del laboratorio." *La Razón*, December 12, 1992.

García, Viviana, and Fernando Martín Peña. "Raúl de la Torre." In *Generaciones 60/90*, edited by Fernando Martín Peña. Buenos Aires: MALBA, 2003: 85–91.

Getino, Octavio. *Cine argentino: Entre lo posible y lo deseable*. Buenos Aires: Fundación Ciccus, 2005.

Gigena, Daniel. "La poesía y el cine de Marilyn Contardi, una habitante de la 'Dublín del sur.'" *La Nación*, December 4, 2018, n. pag. Web.

Giunta, Andrea. *Feminismo y arte latinoamericano: Historias de artistas que emanciparon el cuerpo*. Buenos Aires: Siglo XXI, 2018.

———. "Mujeres entre activismos: Una aproximación comparativa al feminismo artístico en Argentina y Colombia." *Caiana: Revista de Historia del Arte y Cultura Visual del Centro Argentino de Investigadores de Arte* 4 (2014). Web.

———. "Narcisa Hirsch. Portraits." *Alter/Nativas* 1 (Autumn 2013). Web.

Gociol, Judith, and Hernán Invernizzi. *Cine y dictadura: La censura al desnudo*. Buenos Aires: Capital Intelectual, 2006.

Grant, Catherine. "*Intimista* Transformations: María Luisa Bemberg's First Feature Films." In *An Argentine Passion: María Luisa Bemberg and Her Films*, edited by John King, Sheila Whitaker, and Rosa Bosch. New York: Verso, 2000: 73–109.

Graves, Robert. *The Greek Myths*. Vol. 1. Harmondsworth: Penguin Books, 1966.

Guzzante, Mariana. "Abelardo Arias, el agente secreto." *Los Andes. Suplemento cultural*, November 12, 2016. Web.

Halperín Donghi, Tulio. *Vida y muerte de la República verdadera (1910–1930)*. Buenos Aires: Ariel, 2000.

Hardouin, Elodie, and Lilian Laura Ivachow. "Eva, la atrevida." *El Amante Cine* 231 (August 2011): 48–50.

Harvey, David. "The 'New' Imperialism: Accumulation by Dispossession." *Socialist Register* 40 (2004): 63–87.

Hatch, Kristen. "Cutting Women: Margaret Booth and Hollywood's Pioneering Female Film Editors." In *Women Film Pioneers Project*, edited by Jane M. Gaines, Radha Vatsal, and Monica Dall'Asta. Center for Digital Research and Scholarship. New York, NY: Columbia University Libraries, 2013. Web. Accessed April 11, 2019.

Hill, Erin. *Never Done: A History of Women's Work in Media Production*. New Brunswick, NJ: Rutgers UP, 2016.

Holmlund, Chris. "The Eyes of Nelly Kaplan." *Screen* 37, no. 3 (1996): 351–367.

INCAA TV. *En foco: Eva Landeck directora*. Television.

James, Susan. "Complicity and Slavery in *The Second Sex*." In *The Cambridge Companion to Simone de Beauvoir*, edited by Claudia Card. Cambridge: Cambridge UP, 2006: 149–167.

Johnston, Claire. "Women's Cinema as Counter-Cinema." In *Feminism and Film*, edited by E. Ann Kaplan. Oxford: Oxford UP, 2004: 22–33.

"Juguetes en New York." *Clarín*, March 10, 1978.

"Juguetes y Whisky." *Clarín*, April 8, 1978.

Kelly Hopfenblatt, Alejandro. *Modernidad y teléfonos blancos: la comedia burguesa en el cine argentino de los años 40*. Buenos Aires: ENERC-INCAA, 2019.

King, John. "María Luisa Bemberg and Argentine Culture." In *An Argentine Passion: María Luisa Bemberg and Her Films*, edited by John King, Sheila Whitaker, and Rosa Bosch. New York: Verso, 2000: 1–32.

Kriger, Clara. *Cine y Peronismo: El estado en escena*. Buenos Aires: Siglo Veintiuno Editores, 2009.

———. "Cuántas somos en la producción de imágenes y sonido." *Cinémas d'Amérique Latine* 22 (2014). Web.

———. "Gestión estatal en el ámbito de la cinematografía argentina (1933–1943)." *Anuario del Centro de Estudios Históricos "Prof. Carlos S. A. Segreti."* 10, no. 10 (2010): 261–281.

Kruks, Sonia. *Situation and Human Existence: Freedom, Subjectivity, and Society*. London: Unwyn Hyman, 1990.

"La directora Eva Landeck, en el prólogo de otra aventura." *Clarín (Sección Espectáculos)*, July 25, 1977, 33.

Landeck, Eva. *Lejos de Hollywood*. Buenos Aires: Corregidor, 1995.

———. *Máscaras provisorias*. Córdoba: Alción Editora, 2016.

"Las furias." *Heraldo del Cinematografista*, November 9, 1960, 314.

"'Las furias' es una obra pujante y muy original." *La Nación (Sección Espectáculos)*, March 9, 1950, 8.

Lauzen, Martha M. "The Celluloid Ceiling: Behind-the-Scenes Employment of Women on the Top 100, 250, and 500 Films of 2015." *Center for the Study of Women in Television and Film*. 2016. Web. Accessed January 31, 2016.

Listorti, Leandro. "El cortometraje en los 60." In *Generaciones 60/90: Cine argentino independiente*, edited by Fernando Martín Peña. Buenos Aires: MALBA, 2003: 298–305.

Lluch-Prats, Javier. "La Argentina moderna: Mujeres de letras en el entorno del primer centenario de la nación." In *No hay nación para este sexo: La Re(d)pública transatlántica de las Letras: Escritoras españolas y latinoamericanas (1824–1936)*, edited by Pura Fernández. Madrid: Iberoamericano-Vervuert, 2015: 265–284.

López, Daniel. "Vlasta Lah." In *Homenajes I. 31 Festival de Cine de Mar del Plata*, edited by Luis Ormaechea. Buenos Aires: Libros del Festival, 2016: 63–67.

López, Eduardo. *Negro sobre blanco*. (2004). Film.

López Ruiz, Angela. "Resistant Stories." In *Ism Ism Ism: Experimental Cinema in Latin America*, edited by Jesse Lerner and Luciano Piazza. Oakland: U of California P, 2017: 240–263.

"Los nombres prohibidos de la dictadura." *Página/12*, November 16, 2013. Web. Accessed November 6, 2013.

"Los secretos del set." *La Nación*, May 12, 1974, 10–14.

Luraschi, Ilse Adriana, and Kay Sibbald. *María Elena Walsh, o el desafío de la limitación*. Buenos Aires: Sudamericana, 1993.

Lusnich, Ana Laura, and Pablo Piedras, eds. *Una historia del cine político y social en Argentina (1896–1969)*. Buenos Aires: Nueva Librería, 2009.

———. *Una historia del cine político y social en Argentina (1969–2009)*. Buenos Aires: Nueva Librería, 2011.

Mafud, Lucio. *La imagen ausente: El cine mudo argentino en publicaciones gráficas. Catálogo: El cine de ficción, 1914–1923*. Buenos Aires: Editorial Teseo, 2016.

———. "Mujeres cineastas en el período mudo argentino: Los films de las sociedades de beneficencia (1915–1919)." *Imagofagia* 16 (2017): 51–76. Web.

Mahar, Karen Ward. *Women Filmmakers in Early Hollywood*. Baltimore: Johns Hopkins UP, 2006.

Manrupe, Raúl, and María Alejandra Portela. *Un diccionario de films argentinos (1930–1995)*. Buenos Aires: Corregidor, 2001.

Maranghello, César. *Breve historia del cine argentino*. Barcelona: Laertes, 2005.

Margulis, Paola. "Mujeres en el espacio documental: Una apuesta por un campo en vías de conformación." In *Transitos de la mirada: Mujeres que hacen cine*, edited by Paulina Bettendorf and Agustina Pérez Rial. Buenos Aires: Libraria, 2014: 95–114.

"María Elena Walsh en un film lleno de humor, encanto y poesía." *La Nación*, August 20, 1971, 12.

"María Luisa Bemberg y un film feminista." *La Nación*, October 30, 1977.

Marongiu, Federico. 2007. "La ultraderecha en el gobierno justicialista de

1973–1976: Triple A, Juventud Peronista de la República Argentina y Concentración Nacional Universitaria." XI Jornadas Interescuelas/ Departamentos de Historia. Universidad de Tucumán. Web.

Martin, Angela. "Refocusing Authorship in Women's Filmmaking." In *Auteurs and Authorship: A Film Reader*, edited by Barry Keith Grant. Oxford: Blackwell, 2008: 127–134.

Martín, Jorge Abel. "La trayectoria de una pionera: Alicia Míguez Saavedra." *Tiempo Argentino*, April 26, 1983, 12.

Martínez, Adolfo C. "Margarita Bróndolo, un rostro escondido del cine." *La Nación*, December 12, 1992.

Massari, Romina. "El motor sincrónico: El Departamento de cinematografía de la UNLP, su historia." In *Escuela de Cine Universidad Nacional de La Plata: Creación, rescate y memoria*, edited by Romina Massari, Fernando Martín Peña. and Carlos Vallina. La Plata: Universidad Nacional de La Plata, 2006: 11–36.

Mestman, Mariano, and Fernando Martín Peña. "Una imagen recurrente: La representación del Cordobazo en el cine argentino de intervención política." *Colección Breviarios Arte y Libertad* 1 (2005): 21–39.

Ministerio de Cultura y Educación. *Séptimo Festival International de Cine de Cortometraje*. Buenos Aires: Ministerio de Cultura y Educación, 1970.

Montaldo, Graciela. *De pronto, el campo: Literatura argentina y tradición rural*. Rosario: Beatriz Viterbo, 1993.

Moore, Christopher. "Jorge Prelorán: Nativo/extranjero, cineasta/ investigador, conservador/revolucionario, desconocido/vastamente conocido." *Cine Documental* 11 (2015): 75–107.

Mulvey, Laura. "Visual Pleasure and Narrative Cinema." In *Narrative, Apparatus, Ideology*, edited by Philip Rosen. New York: Columbia UP, 1986: 198–209.

Nair, Parvati, and Julián Daniel Gutiérrez-Albilla. "Introduction: Through feminine eyes." In *Hispanic and Lusophone Women Filmmakers: Theory, Practice and Difference*, edited by Parvati Nair, and Julián Daniel Gutiérrez-Albilla. Manchester: Manchester UP, 2013: 1–11.

Nari, Marcela María Alejandra. "No se nace feminista, se llega a serlo: Lecturas y recuerdos de Simone de Beauvoir en Argentina, 1950–1990." *Mora* 8 (2002): 59–72.

"Noticioso." *Heraldo del Cinematografista*, June 15, 1955, 122.

Novaro, Marcos. *Historia de la Argentina, 1955–2010*. Buenos Aires: Siglo Veintiuno Editores, 2010.

Olivera, Guillermo. "Entre lo innombrable y lo enunciable: Visibilidades y espacialidades LGBT en el cine argentino (1960–1991)." In *Estudios queer: Semióticas y políticas de la sexualidad*, edited by F. Forastelli and Guillermo Olivera. Buenos Aires: La Crujía, 2013: 99–111.

Olivera-Williams, María Rosa. *El arte de crear lo femenino: Ficción, género e historia del Cono Sur*. Santiago: Editorial Cuarto Propio, 2012.

Paparella, Aldo. "Almuerzo en la hierba: Entrevista con Narcisa Hirsch sobre el cine experimental argentino." In *Catálogo Narcisa Hirsch*, edited by Alejandra Torres. Buenos Aires: Casa del Bicentenario, Ciudad Autónoma de Buenos Aires, 2010: 63–72.

Pécora, Paolo, and Michelle Ortuno. "Un asunto de mujeres: El rol protagónico de la mujer en el cine argentino." *Cinémas d'Amérique Latine* 17 (2009): 81–92.

Peña, Fernando Martín. *Cien años de cine argentino*. Buenos Aires: Biblos-Fundación OSDE, 2012.

———. "Copete *Las furias* (1960)." *Filmoteca, Temas de cine*. March 24, 2015. Video.

———, ed. *Generaciones 60/90: Cine argentino independiente*. Buenos Aires: MALBA, 2003.

———. "Seminario de mediateca." In *Escuela de Cine Universidad Nacional de La Plata: Creación, rescate y memoria*, edited by Romina Massari, Fernando Martín Peña, and Carlos Vallina. La Plata: Universidad Nacional de La Plata, 2006: 37–98.

Pick, Zuzana. *The New Latin American Cinema: A Continental Project*. Austin: U of Texas P, 1996.

"Por primera vez en la historia del cine argentino una mujer dará la voz de 'Luz, Cámara, Acción' en un film." *La Razón*, June 16, 1960.

Ramanathan, Geetha. *Feminist Auteurs: Reading Women's Films*. London: Wallflower, 2006.

Ramírez Llorens, Fernando. "Empresarios, católicos y Estado en la consolidación del campo cinematográfico en Argentina." *Latin American Research Review* 52, no. 5 (2017): 824–837.

———. *Noches de sano esparcimiento: Estado, católicos y empresarios en la censura al cine en Argentina 1955–1973*. Buenos Aires: Libraria, 2016.

———. "So Close to God, So Close to Hollywood: Catholics and the Cinema in Argentina." *Journal of Latin American Cultural Studies* 23, no. 4 (2014): 325–344.

Rangil, Viviana. *Otro punto de vista: Mujer y cine en la Argentina*. Rosario: Beatriz Viterbo, 2005.

Rich, Adrienne. "Resisting Amnesia: History and Personal Life." In *Blood, Bread, and Poetry: Selected Prose 1979–1985*. New York: Norton, 1986: 136–155.

———. "When We Dead Awaken: Writing as Re-vision." In *On Lies, Secrets, and Silence: Selected Prose 1966–1978*. New York: Norton, 1980: 33–49.

Rodríguez Agüero, Eva, and Alejandra Ciriza. "Viajes apasionados. Feminismos en la Argentina de los 60 y 70." *Labrys études féministes*, July–December 2012. Web. Accessed May 1, 2018.

Rojas, Eduardo. "*Momentos* y *Señora de nadie*: Señores de nadie, nada, nunca." *Revista Canadiense de Estudios Hispánicos* 26, no. 1 (2002): 59–73.

Romero, Luis Alberto. *Breve historia contemporánea de la Argentina*. Buenos Aires: Fondo de Cultura Económica, 1995.

Rosa, María Laura. "El despertar de la conciencia: Impacto de las teorías feministas sobre las artistas de Buenos Aires del '70 y '80." *Artelogie* 5 (September 2013). Web.

Sammaritano, Salvador. "Luchas y proyecciones del corto metraje en la Argentina." *Lyra* 186–188 (1962). N. pag.

———. "Diccionario de la nueva generación argentina: Segunda parte." *Tiempo de Cine* 10/11 (August 1962): 8–12.

———. "Diccionario de la nueva generación argentina." *Tiempo de Cine* 9 (January–March 1962): 3–9.

Santoro, Sonia. "La pionera (Ana Montes)." *Página/12*, August 8, 2003, n. pag.

Sarlo, Beatriz. *La máquina cultural: Maestras, traductores y vanguardistas*. Buenos Aires: Ariel, 1998.

Segunda Muestra Internacional de Cine Independiente. Buenos Aires: Ministerio de Educación y Justicia, Dirección General de Cultura, 1959.

"Se ha Fundado una Escuela de Cine." *Heraldo del Cinematografista*, July 21, 1954, 178.

Seibel, Beatriz. "Mujeres autoras en el cine argentino: Un recuerdo para las pioneras guionistas." *Florencio* 10, no. 40 (July–September 2015): 117–124.

"Se reúnen las furias." *Platea* 1, no. 20 (July 1, 1960): 4–5.

Sibbald, K. M. "María Elena Walsh." In *Encyclopedia of Latin American Literature*, edited by Verity Smith. London: Routledge, 1997: 851–853.

———. "Outing and Autobiography (Carmen Conde and María Elena Walsh)." *Revista Canadiense de Estudios Hispánicos* 35, no. 1 (Autumn 2010): 205–228.

Sigal, Silvia, and Eliseo Verón. *Perón o muerte: Los fundamentos discursivos del fenómeno peronista*. Buenos Aires: Eudeba, 2014.

Silverman, Kaja. *The Acoustic Mirror: The Female Voice in Psychoanalysis and Cinema*. Bloomington: Indiana UP, 1988.

Sitney, P. Adams. *Visionary Film: The American Avant-Garde, 1943–2000*. 3rd edition. New York: Oxford UP, 2002.

Smaldone, Mariana. "Las traducciones rioplatenses de *Le deuxième sexe* de Simone de Beauvoir: Marcas de época en torno a la enunciación de identidades generizadas." *Mutatis Mutandis* 8, no. 2 (2015): 394–416.

Sorensen Goodrich, Diana. *Facundo and the Construction of Argentine Culture*. Austin: U of Texas P, 1996.

Soto, Moira. "La dama del celuloide." *Página/12*, March 9, 2007. Web.

Spadaccini, Silvana. "Carlos Alberto Pessano, de la opinión a la gestión." *Imagofagia* 5 (2012). Web.

Stamp, Shelley. "Women in Early Filmmaking: No Finer Calling." In *Pioneers: First Women Filmmakers*. New York: Kino Lorber, 2018. A Kino Classics Box Set.

Stites Mor, Jessica. "Transgresión y responsabilidad: Desplazamiento de los discursos feministas en cineastas argentinas desde María Luisa Bemberg hasta Lucrecia Martel." In *El cine argentino de hoy: Entre el arte y la política*, edited by Viviana Rangil. Buenos Aires: Biblos, 2007: 137–153.

———. *Transition Cinema: Political Filmmaking and the Argentine Left since 1968*. Pittsburgh: U of Pittsburgh P, 2012.

Strusková, Eva. *The Dodals, Pioneers of Czech Animated Film*. Translated by Lucie Vidmar. Prague: National Film Archive, 2013.

Svampa, Maristella. "Commodities Consensus: Neoextractivism and Enclosure of the Commons in Latin America." *South Atlantic Quarterly* 114, no. 1 (January 2015): 65–82.

———. "El populismo imposible y sus actores, 1973–1976." In *Nueva Historia Argentina, 1955–1976*. Vol. 11, edited by Daniel James. Buenos Aires: Sudamericana, 2003: 381–437.

Tarducci, Mónica. "¿Pero lo leíste en los cincuentas, o más adelante? Memorias de la primera edición argentina de *El Segundo Sexo*." *Doxa: Cuadernos de Ciencias Sociales* 10, no. 20 (1999): 123–130.

Tatar, Maria. "Introduction: Cinderella." In *The Classic Fairy Tales*, edited by Maria Tatar. New York: W. W. Norton, 1999: 101–107.

Trebisacce, Catalina. "Historias feministas desde el lente de María Luisa Bemberg." *Revista Nomadías* 18 (November 2013): 19–41.

Trebisacce, Catalina, and Ana María Veiga. "Variaciones en la trasgresión desde el ojo protésico de María Luisa Bemberg." *Revista Estudos Feministas* 25, no. 3 (September–December 2017): 1405–1417.

Trelles Plazaola, Luis. *Cine y mujer en América Latina: Directoras de largometrajes de ficción*. Río Piedras: Editorial de la Universidad de Puerto Rico, 1991.

Truglio, Marcela. "El cine de las escuelas de cine." In *60/90 Generaciones*, edited by Fernando Martín Peña. Buenos Aires: MALBA, 2003: 308–325.

"Un film con forma y fondo de teleteatro." *La Nación*, October 19, 1963, n. pag.

Uriarte, Claudio. *Almirante Cero: Biografía no autorizada de Emilio Eduardo Massera*. Buenos Aires: Planeta, 2011.

Valles, Rafael. *Fotogramas de la memoria: Encuentros con José Martínez Suárez*. Buenos Aires: Libraria, 2014.

Varea, Fernando G. *El cine argentino durante la dictadura militar, 1976–1983*. Rosario: Editorial Municipal de Rosario, 2008.

Walley, Jonathan. "The Material of Film and the Idea of Cinema: Contrasting Practices in Sixties and Seventies Avant-Garde Film." *October* 103 (Winter 2003): 15–30.

Walsh, María Elena. *Doña Disparate y Bambuco*. Buenos Aires: Alfaguara, 2008.

———. "El cuento de la autora." *Chaucha y Palito*. Buenos Aires: Alfaguara, 2002: 107–132.

Wasertreguer, Silvia, and Hilda Raizman. *La Sala 17: Florencio Escardó y la mirada nueva*. Buenos Aires: Libros del Zorzal, 2009.

Williams, Linda. "Film Bodies: Gender, Genre, and Excess." *Film Quarterly* 44, no. 4 (Summer 1991): 2–13.

Young, Damon R. "The Vicarious Look, or Andy Warhol's Apparatus Theory." *Film Criticism* 39, no. 2 (Winter 2014–2015): 25–52.

Zipes, Jack. "Breaking the Disney Spell." In *The Classic Fairy Tales*, edited by Maria Tatar. New York: W. W. Norton, 1999: 332–352.

Index

Alberti, Mercedes, 106
Aleandro, Norma, 26
Alemann, Marie-Louise, 38, 42
Andes Films, 149n3
André, María Claudia, 83
Andrew, Barbara S., 95, 102–103, 113
Apollon musagète, 22
Aramburu, Pedro Eugenio, 51
Arcadie, 105
Argencolor, 21
Argentina, mayo de 1969: El camino a la liberación (Realizadores de Mayo), 58
Arias, Abelardo, 88, 105–114
Asociación de Cine Experimental, 35, 47, 55
Asociación La Mujer y el Cine, 49
Avellaneda, María Herminia: as filmmaker, 15, 49, 79, 114–122; *Juguemos en el mundo*, 7, 49, 114–122
Azcuénaga, Elena de, 30; *La inundación de Santa Fe*, 30; *Luxación congénita de cadera*, 30; *Opera el profesor Clarence Crafford*, 30; *Quinto dedo varo*, 30
Azules y Colorados, 28–30

Balanchine, George, 22
Beauvoir, Simone de: *The Ethics of Ambiguity*, 81, 84, 87–88, 89–90, 94; *Faut-il brûler Sade?*, 96; reception in Argentine culture generally, 6, 79–84; reception in Argentine films, 84–141, 159n11, 162n26; *The Second Sex*, 81–84, 87–88, 89–105

Bemberg, María Luisa: *Crónica de una señora*, 82–83, 123–124, 137–138, 140–141; feminist activism, 123–141; as filmmaker, 47, 49, 77, 78, 79, 80–81, 104, 123–141, 162n23; influence of Beauvoir on, 82–83, 137–138; *Juguetes*, 83, 136–137, 161n21, 162nn25–26; *Miss Mary*, 139–140; *Momentos*, 7, 83; *El mundo de la mujer*, 83, 125–136, 139–140, 162n24; *Señora de nadie*, 77
Bergoffen, Debra, 90, 95–96
Bernabó, Héctor, 19; *Playa Grande*, 19–20
Bianchi, María Esther, 38; *Las catorce estaciones*, 38
Bianchi, Marta, 49
Birri, Fernando, 23, 30; *Tire dié*, 23, 24
Blanco y negro, 10–11
body genres, 98–99
bombero está triste y llora, El, 38, 48
Borges, Graciela, 82, 137
Borroni, Nelly, 30; *El puente de papel*, 30
Bowlby, John, 25
Brandoni, Luis, 56, 57, 155n34, 156n4
Bredeston, Guillermo, 99
Briski, Norman, 117
Bróndolo, Margarita, 15–18, 152n16
Byrón, Silvestre, 155n31

Caldini, Claudio, 39, 40, 41
Calveiro, Pilar, 66, 69
Cámpora, Héctor, 52, 53
Carballo, Aída, 37–38

179

Carril, Hugo del, 52
Castillo, Alejandra, 91, 101
Catrani, Catrano, 16, 18, 85, 87
Caudillo de la Tercera Posición, El, 52
Cedrón, Lucía, 47
Celestini, María B. de: as feminist filmmaker, 11–12; *Mi derecho*, 10, 11–12, 149n3
celluloid ceiling, 8
censorship, 73–74, 75–77, 147n4, 155n34, 158n12
Centro Experimental de Realización Cinematográfica, 35
Centro Sperimentale, 30, 84
Cinderella, 130–131, 133–136
cineclub, 22–23, 152n20
Cine-Club Núcleo, 23
Cinegraf, 18
Cine Liberación, 131
comedia de fiesta, 147n3
Come out, 43, 44, 45, 148n8
Cómo se hace una película argentina, 13–14
Conde, Mariana Inés, 13, 85, 150n11, 151n14
Contardi, Marilyn, 30, 38, 152n22; *Al sur de Santa Fe*, 152n22; *Jardín de infantes*, 30; *La vieja ciudad*, 30
Cordobazo, 50, 59–60
Cossa, Isabella, 127–128
Crónica de una señora, 82–83, 123–124, 137–138, 140–141
Cuadernos de cine, 24

Daniel, Elsa, 92, 97, 98, 100–101
De la Torre, Raúl: *Crónica de una señora*, 82–83, 123–124, 137–138, 140–141; as filmmaker, 37, 82, 123–124, 140–141
De los abandonados, 24, 25–27
De Ridder, Marcelo, 22
Desanzo, Juan Carlos, 56, 140–141
Descamisado, El, 52
Di Chiara, Roberto, 59
Di Núbila, Domingo, 10
divorce law, 102–103, 159n13

Dodal, Irena: *Apollon musagète*, 22; in Argentina, 21–22; *La reina de las ondas*, 21; in Theresienstadt Ghetto, 21
Dodal, Karel, 21; *La reina de las ondas*, 21
Dorsky, Nathaniel, 39

Editorial Tirso, 88
Encina, Paz, 47
Escardó, Florencio, 25–27
Escuela Cinematográfica Argentina de la Unidad Básica Cultural Eva Perón, 84–85, 158n5
Escuela de Cine de la Universidad de La Plata, 30, 33–35, 37, 154n27
Escuela de Cine Documental de la Universidad de San Martín, 33
Escuela Documental de Santa Fe, 30, 33, 48, 152n22
Ese loco amor loco, 6, 65–74
Estudios San Miguel, 15
Ethics of Ambiguity, The, 81, 84, 87–88, 89–90, 94
experimental film, 22, 38–47, 125–137

Facultad de Filosofía y Letras de la Universidad de Buenos Aires, 54
Faut-il brûler Sade?, 96
Feldman, Norberto, 72
Feldman, Simón, 23, 24
Ferrari, Víctor, 22
Ferraro, Diana, 37; *Primera Exposición Representativa de Artesanías Argentinas*, 37
film schools, 30–35, 54–55
Firestone, Shulamith, 126–127
Fondo Nacional de las Artes, 35–38, 48
Forestal, La, 11, 32
Fradinger, Moira, 10, 151n12
Framini, Andrés, 28
furias, Las, 4, 18, 82, 83–105
furias, Las (play), 88, 92–93, 159n12

Gallo, María Rosa, 38
García de García Mansilla, Angélica, 10; *Un romance argentino*, 10

GEA Cinematográfica, 7, 47
gendered division of labor, 1, 3, 9, 12–18, 78, 85, 150n11; feminized labor, 9, 12–18; negative cutter, 14, 15–18, 152n16; script, la (script girl), 9, 14
Gente en Buenos Aires, 6, 49, 52, 55–65, 72, 73, 75–77, 141, 148n8, 155n34, 156nn2–4
Giberti, Eva, 25–27
Gióvine, Héctor, 68
Giunta, Andrea, 79, 123, 126
Gleyzer, Raymundo, 35, 52; *Los traidores*, 52, 58
Graschinsky, Jaime, 36
Grupo Goethe, 40, 44
Guido, Beatriz, 100–101

hambre oculta, El, 31
Harvey, David, 64
Hill, Erin, 9, 150n11
Hilton, Jorge, 107
Hirsch, Narcisa: *Come out*, 43, 44, 45, 148n8; as filmmaker, 38–47, 148n8; and Grupo Goethe, 38–43; *Homecoming*, 45–47; *Taller*, 43–45; *Testamento y vida interior*, 45
Homecoming, 45–47
Horenstein, Mara, 37; *Aída Carballo y su mundo*, 37
Hospital de Niños Ricardo Gutiérrez, 25–27

Ibsen, Greta, 106
IDHEC (Institut des hautes études cinématographiques), 24
Illia, Arturo, 50
Instituto Cinematográfico del Estado, 18
Instituto di Tella, 35, 41
Instituto Nacional de Cinematografía, 52, 73
Itzcovich, Mabel: *Los caras sucias*, 30; *De los abandonados*, 24, 25–27; as film critic, 24, 30; as filmmaker, 24–30; *Soy de aquí*, 24, 25, 27–30
Ivanissevich, Oscar, 21

Johnston, Claire, 129–130
Juan sin ropa, 10
Juguemos en el mundo, 7, 49, 114–122
Juguetes, 83, 136–137
Juventud Peronista, 32–33, 51–52, 153n25
Juventud Peronista de la República Argentina, 52

Kamín, Bebe, 37; *Los chicos de la guerra*, 37
Kaplan, Nelly, 160n16; *La fiancée du pirate*, 160n16
Kelly Hopfenblatt, Alejandro, 147n3
Kohon, David José, 23; *Buenos Aires* (film), 23; *Prisioneros de una noche*, 63; *¿Qué es el otoño?*, 157n10
Kosice, Gyula, 161n18
Kruks, Sonia, 89–90
Kuhn, Rodolfo, 63; *Los jóvenes viejos*, 63

Lah, Vlasta: as filmmaker, 15, 16, 18, 49, 79, 80; formation as filmmaker, 84–85; *Las furias*, 4, 18, 82, 84–105; *Las modelos*, 18, 83, 86, 88, 105–114
Landeck, Eva: *Barrios y teatros de Buenos Aires*, 35, 55; and censorship, 64–66, 71–77, 156n2, 156n4; *Domingos en Hyde Park*, 35; *El empleo*, 35, 55; *Entremés*, 35, 55; *Ese loco amor loco*, 6, 65–74, 157n11; as filmmaker, 15, 49, 52, 77–78, 140–141; formation as filmmaker, 35, 54–55; *Gente en Buenos Aires*, 6, 49, 52, 55–65, 72, 73, 75–77, 141, 148n8, 155n34, 156nn2–4; *Horas extras*, 35, 55; independent production of films, 55–56, 71–72, 140–141; *El lugar del humo*, 74–77; *Las ruinas de Pompeya*, 35
Lauzen, Martha, 78
Legrin, Juan, 72
Lich (Lichtenstein), Perla, 36–37; *Antonio Pujía*, 36–37
Liga Patriótica Argentina, 11
López Rega, José, 52, 53, 63
lugar del humo, El, 74–77
Lumiton Studios, 86–87
Luz, Aída, 91

Mafud, Lucio, 10–12
Mahar, Karen Ward, 150n11
Mahieu, Agustín, 122
Marino, Heredia, 30; *Feria franca*, 30
Martel, Lucrecia, 47
Martin, Angela, 147n2
Martínez Suárez, José, 23
Massacre, of Trelew, 58
Mayor, Jorge, 116
Mekas, Jonas, 40, 42, 45
Mi derecho, 10, 11–12
Míguez Saavedra, Alicia, 15
modelos, Las, 18, 83, 86, 88, 105–114
Mom, Arturo, 13; *Cómo se hace una película argentina*, 13–14
Momplet, Antonio, 15; *Turbión*, 15
Montes, Ana, 36; *Los Onas: Vida y muerte en Tierra del Fuego*, 36
Montoneros, 51, 52, 57, 58
Morack, Irene, 57, 67
moral compensation, 159n15
Movement of Priests for the Third World, 51
Mugica, Alba, 92, 97, 98
Mulvey, Laura, 98
mundo de la mujer, El, 83, 125–136, 139–140
Murúa, Alfredo, 16
Murúa, Lautaro, 137; *La Raulito*, 112

Nación, La, 73, 93, 113
Nari, Marcela, 81
noche de los bastones largos, la, 50

Obeid, Jorge, 32–33, 154n26
Ocampo, Victoria, 81
Oliver, María Rosa, 81
Olivera, Guillermo, 111
Olivera-Williams, María Rosa, 79–80
Onganía, Juan Carlos, dictatorship of, 34–35, 50, 59, 114, 118–119
Operación Claridad, 70
Operativo Brigadier Estanislao López, 31, 32–33, 153n25

Oroz, Silvia, 33; *Bienamémonos*, 33; *Mayo*, 33; *Los taxis*, 33–34; *La tortura política en argentina, 1966–1972*, 34–35
Ortiz, Mecha, 91

Palant, María Ester, 37; *Cántico de color y luz*, 37; *La conquista de la Pampa*, 37; *Riganelli*, 37
Palant, Pablo, 81
Para Ti, 127–128, 134–135
Peña, Fernando Martín, 86, 123
Perón, Isabel, presidency, 41, 49, 53, 56, 63, 64, 65, 125
Perón, Juan D., 51–53, 64, 118, 125, 153n25, 155n1, 159n13
Peronism: film production under, 13, 22, 23; proscription of, 27–29, 51–53, 118
Peronist resistance, 28
Peronist revolutionary left, 32–33, 51–53, 123, 125, 126, 128, 153n25
Pescadores, 31–32
Pessano, Carlos Alberto, 18–20
Piazzolla, Astor, 86, 97
Playa Grande, 19–20
poder desaparecedor, 66–76
Poliak, Ana, 147n7
Prado, Comandante Manuel, 37
Prat Gay de Constenla, Concepción, 38; *Al corazón de las kenas*, 38; *Allpa Tupak/Tierra prodigiosa*, 38
Prelorán, Mabel, 36
Prelorán, Jorge, 36
primavera camporista (Camporist Spring), 6, 32–33, 50–56, 147n6, 153n25
Producciones Tami, 114
production of film by film schools, 30–35
production of film by Liga Patriótica Argentina, 10–11
production of film by state, 18–20
Pussi, Dolly: as educator, 33; as filmmaker, 30–21, 32–33; *El hambre oculta*, 31; *Pescadores*, 31–32; *Operativo Brigadier Estanislao López*, 31, 32–33, 153n25

Quiroga, Camila, 10

Ramírez Llorens, Fernando, 76, 159n15
Reich, Steve, 43
Renán, Sergio, 56, 112; *La tregua*, 56, 112
Rich, Adrienne, 4, 124, 161n22; on feminist history, 4; on resisting amnesia, 124
Riganelli, Agustín, 37
Rinaldi, Gerardo, 48
Ripoll, Antonio, 48
Ruanova, María, 22
Rumbo Producciones Cinematográficas, 72

Saleny, Emilia: *Delfina*, 10; as educator, 10; as filmmaker, 10, 151n12; *La niña del bosque*, 10; *El pañuelo de Clarita*, 10; *Paseo trágico*, 10
Sammaritano, Salvador, 23
Sánchez Sorondo, Matías G., 19, 20
Sansinena de Elizalde, Elena: *Blanco y negro*, 10–11; film production by Liga Patriótica Argentina, 10–11
Santalla, Perla, 116
Sarandí, 27–30
Sartre, Jean-Paul, 89–90
Second Sex, The, 81–84, 87–88, 89–105
SEGBA power plant fire (1962), 29
Semana Trágica, La, 11
Seminario de Cine, 24
short film, 23–48, 125–137
SIDE Studio, 16
Silverman, Kaja, 43–44
Sitney, P. Adams, 42
Snow, Michael, 42, 43; *A Casing Shelved*, 43
social problem film, 10–11, 12
Sociedad Rural, 62–63, 131, 134, 136, 137
Soffici, Mario, 52
Solanas, Fernando, 128–129; *La hora de los hornos*, 31, 34, 37, 58, 62, 126, 128–129
Sorín, Carlos, 37
Soy de aquí, 24, 25, 27–30

Stamp, Shelley, 9–10
Stantic, Lita: *El bombero está triste y llora*, 48; *Un día*, 48; as filmmaker, 5, 35, 38; *Un muro de silencio*, 48, 148n8; as producer, 5, 7, 47–49, 147n7
state violence in films, 62–63, 65–76
Stravinsky, Igor, 22
Studios Emelco, 22
Suárez de Deza, Enrique, 88, 92–93, 104; *Las furias* (play), 88, 92–93, 159n12
Sur, 81
Svampa, Maristella, 64
synarchy, 52
Szir, Pablo, 38, 48; *El bombero está triste y llora*, 38, 48; *Un día*, 48

Taller, 43–45
Tarducci, Mónica, 81
Tarragona, Rubén, 72
Tato, Miguel Paulino, 53, 65
taxis, Los, 33–34
Temps Modernes, Les (journal), 81
Torre Nilsson, Leopoldo, 100–101; *La casa del ángel*, 100
Torres, Sara, 136
Trebisacce, Catalina, 129
Triángulo de cuatro, 83, 137
Turquetto, Amanda Lucía, 18–20; *Playa Grande*, 18–20

Unión Feminista Argentina (UFA), 83, 123–124, 125–126
Universidad de Tucumán, 36

Valladares, Leda, 115
Viglietti, Daniel, 31
villa miseria (shantytown), 25, 31, 32–33, 35, 57, 63

Walsh, María Elena: as artist and performer, 114–116; *Doña Disparate y Bambuco*, 116; influence of Beauvoir on, 114–115; *Juguemos en el mundo*, 7, 114–122; as scriptwriter, 79

Warhol, Andy, 42
Williams, Linda, 94, 98, 135
Winternitz, Adolfo, 37
World Cup 1978, 70

Young, Damon, 98
Yupanqui, Atahualpa, 62

Zipes, Jack, 134
Zubarry, Olga, 90, 91

About the Author

MATT LOSADA is an associate professor in the Department of Hispanic Studies at the University of Kentucky. He teaches and researches modern Latin American culture, with a particular interest in twentieth-century Argentine film. His first book, *The Projected Nation: Argentine Cinema and the Social Margins*, examined the representation of marginal spaces in Argentine cinema from the 1910s until the present.